The Flying Dutchman

MASTERWORKS OF OPERA

General Editor: Charles Osborne

To Dame Eva Turner
with love and admiration

FRANK GRANVILLE BARKER

The Flying Dutchman

A GUIDE TO THE OPERA

FOREWORD BY
NORMAN BAILEY

BARRIE & JENKINS
COMMUNICA - EUROPA

Designed and produced by Breslich & Foss, London

© Breslich & Foss 1979

First published in 1979 by Barrie & Jenkins
24 Highbury Crescent, London N5 1RX

Design: Craig Dodd
Picture Research: Caroline Lucas and Philippa Lewis

Filmset and printed in Great Britain by
BAS Printers Limited, Over Wallop, Hampshire

ISBN 0 214 20655 6

Contents

Foreword by Norman Bailey

Although the Flying Dutchman was one of the first roles that I ever sang, I am still filled with a profound sense of excitement every time I step on to the stage to perform it anew. Perhaps this is partly due to the islander's instinctive love of the sea linked with our long seafaring heritage, and partly due to the mysterious atmosphere of what has become a classical legend.

In a repertoire, which over the years has ranged from Verdi's Rigoletto and Macbeth to Wagner's Wotan and Hans Sachs, the Flying Dutchman is still one of my most demanding roles. This applies not only vocally (Wagner wrote some very difficult passages for Senta and Erik as well as for the Dutchman), but also in the portrayal of the character. Frank Granville Barker deals in more detail with this particular aspect in his chapter on 'Wagner's Advice to the Players'. From the singer's point of view, Wagner's instructions to the Dutchman requiring him to exercise the utmost economy of movement and gesture, impose a unique type of physical strain. When Senta and the Dutchman meet for the first time and stand virtually motionless for several minutes, the concentrated intensity required by both performers is, in a sense, more exhausting than many more physically active roles.

Throughout the years of singing this role I have experienced many unusual performances including several when Senta, with her back to the audience in the above-mentioned scene, used to cross her eyes to try to make me laugh. I have had a Daland who went so completely hoarse in the first act that the whole of the second act aria was sung an astonishing octave deeper, and I have performed with an Erik so drunk that what he sang had not the slightest connection with what Wagner had written! For those performances one could literally say that it was like starting off on a voyage into the unknown!

Wotan (including the Wanderer) and the Dutchman occupy

unique positions in the Wagnerian baritone (*Heldenbariton*) repertoire—to sing them does not make a *Heldenbariton*, but conversely he cannot be truly called one without these roles in his repertoire. Although the Wagnerian style is distinctive, the vocal technique must remain Italian. This, for me, is the golden rule which the Wagnerian singer breaks at his or her peril!

No operatic composer has so consistently achieved a more perfect marriage between the orchestral sound and vocal line, and singing the big Wagnerian roles is one of the great human experiences.

Norman Bailey

The Flying Dutchman

OPERA IN THREE ACTS BY

RICHARD WAGNER

Background to the Opera

There is no convenient rule governing the way in which composers have chosen the dramatic material for their operas. Sometimes the nature of the libretto has been determined by the particular occasion for which the opera was commissioned, while in other instances the composer has accepted the first subject thrust upon him, either through laziness or because he simply needed to earn some money. In other cases the composer has made his own choice: having read a poem or seen a play, he has felt inspired to set it to music because of the power of its theme or the fascination of one or more of its characters. He would then choose a librettist to prepare a text according to his own instructions. Similarly, composers have varied in their manner of treating their texts: some have set the verses as they stood, while others have collaborated with the librettist every inch of the way. Usually operas have been completed quite quickly once the subject has been decided and the libretto prepared, but there are cases where a long period has elapsed between the original sparking of the composer's imagination and his beginning work on the music. Wagner's *Der fliegende Holländer* (*The Flying Dutchman*) is a particularly interesting case in point.

Opposite: The house in Leipzig where Richard Wagner was born on May 22, 1813

Overleaf: A gathering of the faithful at the Villa Wahnfried: Cosima Wagner with young Siegfried; Wagner holding a score; Liszt at the piano, with a portrait of King Ludwig above him

It was during the summer of 1838 that the idea of *The Flying Dutchman* first arose in Wagner's mind, yet he did not write his first sketch for a libretto until 1840. Even so, another full year was to pass before he settled down to write his 'poem' in its final form, then compose the music in the space of seven weeks, leaving only the orchestration and the overture to be completed in the winter months of 1841. It seems remarkable that Wagner should carry the idea for an opera in his head for three whole years and then dash off words and music with such speed. We should be grateful for his delay, however, because had he composed *The Flying Dutchman* on that first impulse in 1838 it would have been a different, much inferior work to the one he

Right: Drawing of Wagner by Ernst Kietz, a close and loyal friend during the difficult days in Paris, where The Flying Dutchman *was composed. The young painter was so indolent that he rarely finished a portrait, but the pencil sketch he made of Wagner in 1839 was almost completed two years later*

eventually gave us. He did not spend any great deal of time composing during the three intervening years, but he went through a variety of experiences which changed his entire outlook on opera and gave birth to the conviction that he had a mission to perform. It is necessary to know something about these experiences in order to appreciate the revolutionary nature of *The Flying Dutchman* and the reasons why Wagner took this first step along the road from opera to music drama.

Although his development subsequent to *The Flying Dutchman* followed a logical course as he gradually perfected his grand design to synthesise the arts into a unified whole, a form of music drama that would illuminate the souls of the characters rather than their actions and emotions, Wagner began his creative career in a chaotically haphazard manner. As a boy he was taught the rudiments of piano playing, but it was of little interest to him: his passion was for the theatre, as dramatist rather than actor. He displayed a genuine gift for writing verse, even winning the satisfaction of having one of his schoolboy poems published. So far as music was concerned he was content to use his limited ability to play the piano as a means of exploring music for the poetic and dramatic images it evoked. He was virtually self-taught, submitting himself in his late teens to little more than a year's formal education in music. That he possessed a natural talent, however, is proved by the fact that at the age of nineteen, with a symphony and three concert overtures to his credit, he was appointed chorus master of the opera company at Würzburg. A little over a year later, in July 1834, he became conductor of a company with its headquarters in Magdeburg.

Already, then, Wagner had decided to make his career in the opera house, and the completion of his first opera, *Die Feen* (*The Fairies*), at the beginning of 1834 indicated that his ultimate ambition lay in composition. The projected production of this opera in Leipzig, incidentally, was abandoned because the theatre director did not favour its imitation of Weber and Marschner, and it remained unperformed until 1888. It has rarely been revived, and frankly does not deserve to be. A second opera, *Das Liebesverbot* (*The Ban on Love*), which secured a single performance at Magdeburg in 1836, was more in the style of Bellini and Auber. So although Wagner had made up his mind to become an opera composer, he appeared to be uncertain as to which tradition he should follow. His abrupt switch from a native to an Italian style, moreover, contradicts all our ideas of him as the eloquent champion of German art.

The reason for Wagner's attraction to the Italian style of opera at this time is made clear in articles he contributed to several journals. In these, the earliest of his theoretical writings, he gave due credit to German composers for their superior instrumental compositions, but cast serious doubts on their ability to compete with the Italians when it came to opera. 'We are too intellectual', he argued in one of his articles, 'to create warm human figures. Mozart could do so, because he enlivened his characters with the beauty of Italian song. Since we have come to despise this, we have strayed further and further from the path that Mozart made for the salvation of our dramatic music. Weber never knew how to handle song, nor does Spohr understand it much better. But song is the instrument through which a human being can communicate himself musically, and so long as this is not fully developed he lacks genuine speech.' He goes on to emphasise that beauty of song is second nature to the Italian composer, quoting Bellini as the perfect example. Quite recently, he specifies, he had seen a performance of *I Capuleti e i Montecchi* and had been overwhelmed by hearing simple, noble song in place of the 'allegorising orchestral bustle' of German opera. The Romeo in that performance, it is fascinating to note, was Wilhelmine Schröder-Devrient, who was to become the first Senta in *The Flying Dutchman*.

Another reason for Wagner's turning his back on the specifically German style of Weber and his followers was that in his capacity as conductor at various minor operas in Germany and at Riga (1837–39) he discovered that the public was almost unanimous in its preference for Italian opera. Just like him, in fact, audiences craved for melody above all else. His practical experience made it clear to him that for any composer to succeed his operas must be in the style which the leading European houses demanded. With his eye on Paris, then the operatic capital of the world, he realised that stage spectacle was equally important, so it was natural that he should look for an example to Meyerbeer. Here was a German composer who had been astute enough to take the Italian and French schools as his models and beat them at their own game. Wagner even wrote to Meyerbeer from Riga in 1837 to congratulate him on the course he had taken, the only course which would enable German opera composers to create masterpieces. (There is immense irony here, for he was later to condemn Meyerbeer with the most vindictive savagery both as man and artist.) In this letter he also goes to the extent of expressing regret for his enthusiasm for Beethoven.

The obviously confused state of Wagner's thoughts at this time is due in great part to his living abroad, out of touch with his German fellow-composers. He had taken up his post in Riga, a city then as now under Russian rule, chiefly to escape from his creditors. Although he had so far shown only a promising talent for music, he had already proved the genius for falling into debt that was to distinguish him all his life. The time

in Riga was not wasted, however, for it was there that he
composed the first two acts of *Rienzi*, a grand opera inspired by
Bulwer Lytton's novel, and read the story of *The Flying
Dutchman* in a book of imaginary memoirs by Heinrich Heine.
Already familiar with this popular legend of a ship's captain
condemned to sail the seas until Judgment Day, Wagner was
only prompted to give it any serious attention after reading
Heine's individual treatment of it. 'This subject', he commented
later, 'attracted me and made an indelible impression on my
mind; yet at the time it did not gather enough force to compel
me into using it creatively.' That force was to build up gradually
over the following three years.

In the spring of 1839 Wagner was given notice of dismissal from his post in Riga, which was to take effect in the summer. He saw this action, as he saw every setback he suffered during his stormy career, as an act of treachery on the part of his colleagues, though in fact he had only himself to blame. He had made no secret of his contempt for the greater part of the theatre's repertoire, which did nothing to endear him to its director, staff and artists. There were no grounds for complaint so far as the quantity or quality of his work was concerned, because he had maintained the highest possible standards in the fifteen operas he had prepared for his first season and the twenty-four for his second, but he had forced the company into reckless expense to achieve these standards. The most serious factor of all, however, was that he was in debt all over the town, and it was only a matter of time before his creditors would close in, making the theatre the centre of a scandal.

In spite of all his predictable expressions of indignation, it is most likely that Wagner was relieved by the prospect of moving on from Riga, which he had outgrown by that time. His first problem was to decide where to go in furtherance of his ambitions. Whatever feelings he might have held concerning his homeland, a return to Germany was ruled out on artistic and practical grounds. The theatres there followed the example of Italy and Paris, the latter in particular, so he could not hope for any success at home until he had made his name abroad. On a more mundane level, going back to Germany would immediately expose him to the hungry packs of creditors waiting for him in every city where he had lived and worked. Paris was the more attractive choice, since he believed he would secure the help there of Meyerbeer, whose influence was boundless and who would doubtless respect the composer of *Rienzi*, which Wagner hoped to complete in a few months' time.

Having solved this first problem, and secured his wife Minna's assent, there remained the question of how to elude his creditors in Riga. Russian law did not permit the granting of a passport to anyone proposing to leave the country until that person had given notice of his intention in local newspaper advertisements. Since the last thing he wanted was to let anyone in Riga know he was leaving, Wagner worked out a plan to cross the border illicitly. He was helped in the first place by the company's playing a short season in Mitau, a town closer to the

Prussian border. Having conducted several performances there as though everything were normal, he left quietly one day in a carriage with Minna and their New Foundland dog, Robber. After two days they reached the Russo-Prussian border and the most dangerous part of their escape.

'A few hundred feet away', Wagner recalled in his autobiography, 'on the slope of a hill, lay the ditch which ran the whole length of the frontier, watched continually and at very narrow intervals by Cossacks. Our chance was to utilise the few moments after the relief of the watch, during which the sentries were engaged elsewhere. We had to run at full speed down the hill, scramble through the ditch, and then hurry along until we were beyond the range of the soldiers' guns; for the Cossacks were bound in case of discovery to fire upon us even on the other side.' The next stage of their journey, which would fit quite happily into the plot of any adventure story of the period, was a sea voyage from the Prussian port of Pillau to London. Wagner decided upon this course out of consideration for Robber: 'to convey him to Paris by coach was out of the question' is his throw-away line at this point in his narrative. And so it was his concern for a dog which brought about Wagner's second vital step towards *The Flying Dutchman*.

The voyage started with the Wagners, lacking the necessary passports, having to board the *Thetis*, a small merchant vessel, by stealth and hide below deck to escape the notice of harbour officials. Everything passed smoothly until the ship was sailing through the Cattegat, when a violent storm blew up. The captain was finally obliged to seek shelter at a harbour on the Norwegian coast, where Wagner found a scene that would become the setting of the first act of *The Flying Dutchman*. 'What I had taken to be a continuous line of cliffs', he wrote, 'turned out on our approach to be a series of separate rocks projecting from the sea. The hurricane was so broken by the rocks in our rear that the further we sailed through this ever-changing labyrinth of projecting rocks, the calmer the sea became. A feeling of indescribable content came over me when the enormous granite walls echoed the hail of the crew as they cast anchor and furled the sails. The sharp rhythm of this call clung to me like an omen of good cheer, and shaped itself presently into the theme of the seamen's song in my *Fliegende Holländer*. The idea of this opera was, even at that time, ever present in my mind, and it now took on a definite poetic and musical colour under the influence of my recent impressions.'

The *Thetis* took to sea again two days later, its captain ignoring the pilot's warning of further bad weather, and within a few hours, while the Wagners were 'in the act of eating a lobster for the first time in our lives', almost foundered on a reef. The ship was taken to another Norwegian harbour for the damage to be inspected, then set sail again after a day's delay. Their tribulations were not over, however, for a few days later, on August 6, the wind changed and an even more violent storm began to rage. 'On the 7th', Wagner continues, 'at half-past two in the afternoon, we thought ourselves in imminent danger of

Below: German wood engraving of terrified ship's crew sighting the Dutchman's ghostly vessel

death. It was not the terrible force with which the vessel was hurled up and down, entirely at the mercy of this sea monster, which appeared now as a fathomless abyss, now as a steep mountain peak, that filled me with mortal dread; my premonition of some terrible crisis was aroused by the despondency of the crew, whose malignant glances seemed to point to us as the cause of threatening disaster. Ignorant of the trifling occasion for the secrecy of our journey, the thought may have occurred to them that our need of escape had arisen from suspicious or even criminal circumstances.'

By curious and totally unforseeable chance, Wagner was experiencing at first hand some of the elements which made up the story of *The Flying Dutchman*. There was nothing supernatural about these events, no defiant captain's vow to hold his course even if it meant sailing the seas until the Day of Judgment, no attendant curse and promise of an unlikely form of redemption from it. Nevertheless, Wagner discovered what it meant to be at the mercy of the storm, and was brought face to face with the antagonism of a crew which believed that a crime committed by someone on board a ship might cause its destruction and the loss of their own lives. The captain, moreover, though he bore no resemblance to the ill-fated Dutchman, had at least displayed an obstinate rejection of his pilot's advice. Poor Minna, who must have wondered how she had ever become involved in such a melodramatic adventure, supplied an additional touch to the story. 'Minna', the composer recalled, 'expressed the fervent wish to be struck by lightning with me rather than to sink, living, into the fearful flood.' Unconsciously, she was expressing Senta's desire to sacrifice herself for the Dutchman in the future opera.

More than three weeks after leaving Pillau the Wagners arrived in London with their long-suffering dog. Taking eight days' rest before continuing their journey to Paris, they spent an afternoon in the strangers' gallery of the House of Lords listening to a debate, no doubt a pleasantly somnolent experience after their adventures at sea. (Wagner also strikes a familiar chord when he observed: 'We shuddered through a ghastly London Sunday.') The Channel crossing brought an unexpected stroke of good fortune. Wagner made the acquaintance on the ship of two ladies who were friends of Meyerbeer and who were kind enough, knowing that the great

man was then in Boulogne, to give him a letter of introduction. When Wagner called on him, Meyerbeer graciously listened to him read the first three acts of his *Rienzi* libretto and promised to recommend him to the manager and the conductor of the Paris Opéra.

Opposite: The London boarding house where Wagner broke his journey to Paris

When Wagner at last arrived in Paris on September 17, 1839, he was confident that he would conquer this most important of all musical citadels. He was undeterred by the rejection of *Die Feen* and the failure of *Das Liebesverbot*, because he had absolute faith in *Rienzi*, of which he still had three acts to compose. Disillusionment quickly set in, however, as he discovered that Paris was a materialistic, decidedly frivolous city, the leaders of whose musical establishment had no interest whatsoever in the new artistic ideas of an ambitious young German. He found himself obliged to earn a meagre living from kinds of work he had never imagined himself doing. One, which he found particularly irksome, was producing arrangements of the very operas he most despised. Of Donizetti's *La favorite*, he was asked to concoct no fewer than six different complete arrangements: for voice and piano, for piano solo, for piano duet, for a quartet, for two violins and for cornet. The far more important new work he embarked upon was his contribution of articles to the *Gazette musicale*.

His Paris writings are delightful in themselves, revealing a bright and witty side to his character which is sadly absent from his later, more serious essays on aesthetics. These articles had a special value, moreover, in that they made him think about the musical scene around him and focus his attention on its failings. They testify to his mounting dissatisfaction with the type of operas currently being composed and the way in which they were presented, then to his return to his original admiration for Beethoven, and finally to his gradual development of a theory of music drama which would raise opera into a new and far more significant art-form. He does not argue his case in an academic way, however, but employs fiction and satire as well as direct reporting to drive his points home, many of which were clearly leading him slowly yet inevitably towards *The Flying Dutchman*.

The youthful Wagner had disparaged German opera in seeking to prove the superiority of the Italian style which was founded on simple yet expressive melody, and in his letter to Meyerbeer he had even appeared to turn his back on Beethoven.

Now, in Paris, he completely reversed his attitude. In the story 'A Pilgrimage to Beethoven', serialised in the Paris journal during November and December 1840, he gives his first hint of the mission he intended to take on. His fictional pilgrim describes to Beethoven a recent performance of *Fidelio* he had attended in Vienna.

'That was a tiresome labour', the surly composer replies. 'I am no opera composer—by which I mean there is not a single theatre in the world for which I would willingly write another opera. Any opera that I would write after my own heart would make people run away. Operas today are patched together out of arias, duets and terzettos, which I would replace by music no singer would want to perform and no audience would want to hear. All they understand now is dazzling lies and sugary trash. Anyone who composed a real musical drama would be dismissed as an idiot.' Asked by his visitor how he would go to work on a musical drama, Beethoven explains: 'As Shakespeare did when he wrote his plays. The composers today who are content to supply the kind of vocal nonsense with which any nonentity can win himself an ovation would be better employed dress-making in Paris.'

It is quite clear here that Wagner is putting his own opinions into the mouth of the Beethoven of this imaginary interview. He goes even further when he makes the old composer propose a music of the future. 'Why should not vocal music be regarded as equally great and serious as instrumental music? The human voice is a nobler and more expressive organ than any orchestral instrument, so why should it be handled less independently.' He goes on to make the point that while instruments represent the primal aspects of creation and nature, the voice represents the human heart and the individual sensibility. If only the orchestra and the voice could be brought together in the right spirit, each making its optimum contribution to drama, then a whole new creative world would be opened up. A purely Wagnerian principle is set out when Beethoven comments *à propos* his Ninth Symphony, that the 'Ode to Joy' by Schiller which he drew upon for the last movement is a very uplifting poem, yet a long way from expressing the ideas represented in the music. Wagner is emphasising yet again his belief that the composer intending to create true music drama must always be his own librettist.

Another distinctly autobiographical note is sounded in the story 'Death in Paris'. Here the central character, whose identity remains a mystery, declares his artistic credo in his dying hour. 'I believe in God, Mozart and Beethoven, likewise in their disciples and apostles; I believe in the Holy Ghost and in the one and indivisible Art. ... I believe in a Day of Judgment when all who dared to exploit this true and noble art for the sake of profit, dishonouring and disgracing it for the sake of sensual pleasure, will be terribly punished.' The 'indivisible Art' is the music drama which Wagner was determined to create in the place of traditional opera, and which he was to introduce, albeit without complete certainty or consistency, in *The Flying Dutchman*. The hero's credo, incidentally, was gratefully seized upon by Bernard Shaw, a fervent Wagnerite, for the painter Dubedat in his play *The Doctor's Dilemma* sixty-five years later. (The chief difference was that Dubedat omitted to express any belief in God, which outraged the critics as well as the audiences of the time.)

Wagner's own musical work had progressed slowly in the meantime, though he had finally completed the score of *Rienzi* in November, 1840. Originally he had intended this spectacular work—once described, wittily though not accurately, as 'the best opera Meyerbeer did *not* compose'—for the Paris Opéra. 'I soon discovered', he confessed in a letter of the period, 'that I should have to wait two or three years before I could have a big work of this kind produced in Paris, for I should first have to make myself known by some smaller operas. So I decided to complete it in German with a view to a German theatre. I selected Dresden, because it is in a sense my native town, and I have made every kind of preparation, especially with Meyerbeer's help, to ensure the opera's being presented there.' He even sent a letter to King Friedrich August of Saxony, begging him to order the production of *Rienzi* in Dresden. In June of the following year the management of the opera house at Dresden accepted the opera for production, promising to put it on at the beginning of 1842, though in fact its première did not take place until the October of that year.

While composing the music for *Rienzi*, Wagner began sketching out a first plan for *The Flying Dutchman*. He wrote it in a single act, convinced that in this way he could confine the drama to the developing relationships between the principal

Opposite: Charlotte Saunders in the title role of The Flying Dutchman; or The Demon Seaman and the Lass That Loved a Sailor, *a burlesque by William Brough presented at the Royalty Theatre, London, in 1869*

27

characters without troubling about what he called the 'tiresome accessories' of traditional opera. There was also a practical reason for this decision: 'I thought I could rely', he wrote later, 'on a better prospect for the acceptance of my proposed work if it were cast in the form of a one-act opera, such as was frequently given as a curtain raiser before a ballet at the Grand Opera.' (There is something delightfully incongruous in the idea of a Wagner opera acting as a curtain raiser to a ballet.) He again went for help to Meyerbeer, who took him in the summer of 1840 to meet Léon Pillet, the new director of the Opéra. He was mortified when the outcome of this conference was nothing more than the suggestion that he should begin by co-operating with some other composer in writing a scene for a ballet. His only consolation was that Pillet agreed to look over his *Flying Dutchman* sketch.

Months of wretchedness followed for Wagner, who had come to Paris with such high hopes. While he waited for news concerning the fate of *Rienzi* he carried on with his various forms of hack work to eke out a living, encouraged only by the devotion of Minna. Their household was run so meagrely that Robber had left to find a better home for himself, proving that even canine loyalty has its limits. Then in the early summer of 1841 Wagner learnt that Pillet, having taken a liking to the sketch of *The Flying Dutchman*, wanted to buy the plot to give to another composer. The irate Wagner tried to explain that he alone could treat the subject worthily and that it was his original idea in the first place, but he met with no success. Pillet bluntly informed him that he could not commission an opera from Wagner for the next seven years, as his existing contracts would cover that period. Having sought the advice of his friend Edouard Monnaie, the editor of the *Gazette musicale*, Wagner finally agreed, and in the event Pillet paid him quite generously for his plot, which was subsequently turned by two French scribblers into a libretto with the title *Le vaisseau fantôme* for the composer Pierre Dietsch.

It was this unexpected windfall which finally prompted Wagner to compose the music for his own *Flying Dutchman*, leaving *Le vaisseau fantôme* to sail itself on to the rocks. He had already completed the full version of the poem in May, and with Pillet's fee of five hundred francs providing a period of comparative leisure, he finally put his whole mind to the work

Left: A page of the libretto of The Flying Dutchman *in Wagner's handwriting, dated May 19, 1841*

Right: The Court Theatre in Dresden, where Rienzi *was produced in 1842, followed by* The Flying Dutchman *in 1843*

which had first fired his imagination three years earlier, and which had been stimulated by personal experience during the stormy crossing from Pillau to London. Everything fell into place so easily that he composed the entire work, in its unorchestrated form, within seven weeks during August and September. After a short break he was able to resume work, and by the beginning of December had actually sent off the score to Berlin, where he hoped for a prestigious production. Again the kindly Meyerbeer lent his support.

Meyerbeer's generous behaviour towards Wagner should be emphasised, because the ungrateful young composer was later to vilify his benefactor and even deny that he had helped him in any way. The diary of Meyerbeer carries an entry for December 7, 1841, which reads: 'Called on Redern [the Intendant of the opera house] to recommend to him the score of *Der fliegende Holländer*.' Two days later he wrote a letter to Redern including the following recommendation: 'The day before yesterday I had the honour to speak to your Excellency about this interesting composer, whose talent and extremely straitened circumstances make him doubly worthy of not having the doors of the great Court Theatre that is the protector of German art closed to him.' Similarly, Meyerbeer had already proved his good intentions towards Wagner by recommending *Rienzi* to the management in Dresden. 'Herr R. Wagner', he had written, 'is a young composer who has not only a sound musical training

16ᵗᵉ Vorstellung im ersten Abonnement.
Königlich Sächsisches Hoftheater.

Donnerstag, den 20. October 1842.

Zum ersten Male:

Rienzi,
der Letzte der Tribunen.

Große tragische Oper in 5 Aufzügen von Richard Wagner.

Personen

Cola Rienzi, päpstlicher Notar.	—	Herr Tichatscheck.
Irene, seine Schwester.	—	Dem. Wüst.
Steffano Colonna, Haupt der Familie Colonna.	—	Herr Dettmer.
Adriano, sein Sohn.	—	Mad. Schröder-Devrient.
Paolo Orsini, Haupt der Familie Orsini.	—	Herr Wächter.
Raimondo, Abgesandter des Papstes in Avignon.	—	Herr Vestri.
Baroncelli, } römische Bürger.	—	{Herr Reinhold
Cecco del Vecchio, }	—	{Herr Risse.
Ein Friedensbote.	—	Dem. Thiele.

Gesandte der lombardischen Städte, Neapels, Baierns, Böhmens rc. Römische Nobili,
Bürger und Bürgerinnen Rom's, Friedensboten. Barmherzige Brüder. Römische Trabanten.
Rom um die Mitte des vierzehnten Jahrhunderts.

Die im zweiten Akt vorkommenden Solotänze werden ausgeführt von den Damen: Pecci-
Ambrogio, Benoni und den Herren Ambrogio und Balletmeister Lepitre.

Der Text der Gesänge ist an der Casse für 3 Neugroschen zu haben.

Einlaß-Preise:

Ein Billet in die Logen des ersten Ranges und das Amphitheater . .	1 Thlr.	10 Ngr.
" " " " Fremdenlogen des zweiten Ranges Nr. 1. 14. und 29.	1 "	10 "
" " " " übrigen Logen des zweiten Ranges	— "	25 "
" " " " Sperr-Sitze der Mittel- u. Seiten-Gallerie des dritten Ranges	— "	15 "
" " " " Mittel- und Seiten-Logen des dritten Ranges . . .	— "	12¼ "
" " " " Sperr-Sitze der Gallerie des vierten Ranges	— "	10 "
" " " " Mittel-Gallerie des vierten Ranges	— "	8 "
" " " " Seiten-Gallerie-Logen daselbst	— "	6 "
" " " " Sperr-Sitze im Cercle.	— "	25 "
" " " " Parterre-Logen	— "	25 "
" " " das Parterre	— "	15 "

Die Billets sind nur am Tage der Vorstellung gültig, und zurückgebrachte Billets werden nur bis
Mittag 12 Uhr an demselben Tage angenommen.

Der Verkauf der Billets gegen sofortige baare Bezahlung findet in der, in dem untern
Theile des Rundbaues befindlichen Expedition, auf der rechten Seite, nach der Elbe zu, früh
von 9 bis Mittags 12 Uhr und Nachmittags von 3 bis 4 Uhr statt.

Alle zur heutigen Vorstellung bestellte und zugesagte Billets sind Vormittags von 9 Uhr bis
längstens 11 Uhr abzuholen, außerdem darüber anders verfüget wird.

Der freie Einlaß beschränkt sich bei der heutigen Vorstellung blos auf die
zum Hofstaate gehörigen Personen und die Mitglieder des Königl. Hoftheaters.

Einlaß um 5 Uhr. Anfang um 6 Uhr.
Ende um 10 Uhr.

Left: Playbill for the première of Rienzi *at the Court Theatre, Dresden, on October 20, 1842*

Below: Scene from the original production of Rienzi, *a grand opera in the style of Meyerbeer which was enthusiastically received by the Dresden audience*

but also much imagination and a general musical culture; and his situation deserves the sympathy of his fatherland in each of these aspects. . . . Some sections of this opera that he played to me I found full of fantasy and of considerable dramatic effect. May the young artist be able to rejoice in the protection of your Excellency, and find an opportunity to see his fine talent more generally recognised.'

Wagner was informed in February 1842 that *The Flying Dutchman* had been accepted for production in Berlin, and with two stage successes to look forward to in the near future he felt the time was ripe to leave Paris, which he had come to loathe during his two and a half years there. At last he could return to Germany to prepare for the triumphs he was confident that *Rienzi* and *The Flying Dutchman* would bring him. Minna, too, was delighted at the prospect of returning to their homeland. They left the French capital on April 7, arriving in Dresden five days later. The rest of the year was taken up with preparations for the performance of *Rienzi*, which finally took place in

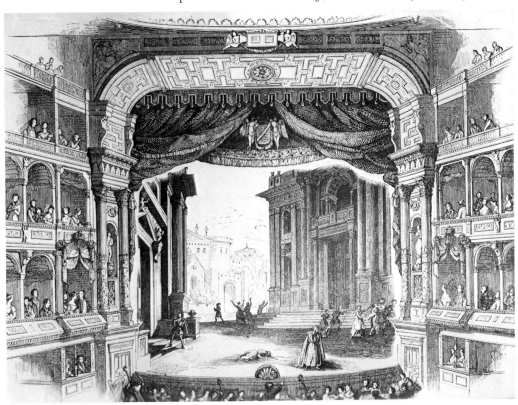

Dresden on October 20, and with constant attempts to secure an early performance of *The Flying Dutchman* in Berlin. The latter appeared the more important to Wagner because, while a success in Dresden might or might not impress the rest of Germany, a success in Berlin would certainly do so, bringing fame and fortune with it. He was assured that his work would be staged there immediately after the theatre's projected production of Meyerbeer's *Huguenots* that year.

Nothing ever ran smoothly for Wagner, however, so that even when *Rienzi* proved a spectacular triumph the management in Berlin continued to drag its feet. He found himself an overnight celebrity with *Rienzi*, which became a long-running success such as Dresden had rarely experienced. Not unnaturally, the theatre there sought the *cachet* of presenting the première of *The Flying Dutchman* as well. Wagner tried desperately to make the management in Berlin put on this work immediately, but he was told that it could not be staged until the following February, as an opera by Lachner had a prior claim. Wagner's high-handed reply was that if *The Flying Dutchman* was not produced at once the score must be returned to him for performance in Dresden, offering on his part to send it back to Berlin in time for the promised February production there. The score was duly returned to him, rehearsals began straight away, and *The Flying Dutchman* had its première at the Dresden Court Theatre on January 2, 1843.

To the composer's utter dismay, it was a failure. The immediate reason was that the audience, which had been so stimulated by the brilliance of the more superficial *Rienzi*, was dismayed by the gloomy subject of the new work, 'ghastly pallid' being one comment which summed up the general reaction. There was also one grave weakness in the casting. Wilhelmine Schröder-Devrient, who understood a good deal of what Wagner was trying to do with this revolutionary work, sang and acted with the utmost conviction as Senta, but Johann Michael Wächter showed himself to be all at sea, in the wrong sense, as the Dutchman. Then there was the failure of the settings to do anything like justice to Wagner's conception of the work, in which scenery and acting were as important as the musical element. This was not really surprising, since in the rush to stage *The Flying Dutchman* the sets were taken over piecemeal from existing productions, the cyclorama for Act I

1ste Vorstellung im vierten Abonnement.

Königlich Sächsisches Hoftheater.

Montag, den 2. Januar 1843.

Zum ersten Male:

Der fliegende Holländer.

Romantische Oper in drei Akten, von Richard Wagner.

Personen:

Daland, norwegischer Seefahrer.	Herr Risse.
Senta, seine Tochter.	Mad. Schröder-Devrient.
Erik, ein Jäger.	Herr Reinhold
Mary, Haushälterin Dalands.	Mad. Wächter.
Der Steuermann Dalands.	Herr Bielczizky.
Der Holländer.	Herr Wächter.

Matrosen des Norwegers. Die Mannschaft des fliegenden Holländers. Mädchen.

Scene: Die norwegische Küste.

Textbücher sind an der Casse das Exemplar für 2½ Neugroschen zu haben.

Krank: Herr Dettmer.

Einlaß-Preise:

	Thlr.	Ngr.
Ein Billet in die Logen des ersten Ranges und das Amphitheater	1	—
Fremdenlogen des zweiten Ranges Nr. 1. 14. und 29.	1	—
übrigen Logen des zweiten Ranges	—	20
Sperr-Sitze der Mittel- u. Seiten-Gallerie des dritten Ranges	—	12½
Mittel- und Seiten-Logen des dritten Ranges	—	10
Sperr-Sitze der Gallerie des vierten Ranges	—	8
Mittel-Gallerie des vierten Ranges	—	7½
Seiten-Gallerie-Logen daselbst	—	5
Sperr-Sitze im Cercle.	—	20
Parterre-Logen	—	15
das Parterre	—	10

Die Billets sind nur am Tage der Vorstellung gültig, und zurückgebrachte Billets werden nur bis Mittag 12 Uhr an demselben Tage angenommen.

Der Verkauf der Billets gegen sofortige baare Bezahlung findet in der, in dem untern Theile des Rundbaues befindlichen Expedition, auf der rechten Seite, nach der Elbe zu, früh von 9 Uhr bis Mittags 12 Uhr, und Nachmittags von 3 bis 4 Uhr statt.

Alle zur heutigen Vorstellung bestellte und zugesagte Billets sind Vormittags von 9 Uhr bis längstens 11 Uhr abzuholen, außerdem darüber anders verfüget wird.

Der freie Einlaß beschränkt sich bei der heutigen Vorstellung blos auf die zum Hofstaate gehörigen Personen und die Mitglieder des Königl. Hoftheaters.

Einlaß um 5 Uhr.   Anfang um 6 Uhr.

Ende gegen 9 Uhr.

from *Oberon*, the hulls of the ships from a ballet called *Der Seeräuber*, the room in Daland's house from *Faust*, and the exterior of the house in Act III from *William Tell*.

After four performances *The Flying Dutchman* was taken out of the repertoire, though Wagner at least had the satisfaction of seeing his *Rienzi* put into its place. He may well have understood the true reason for this, as we all know it today: *The Flying Dutchman* was ahead of its time. As the years went by, the early spectacular opera fell by the wayside and the later, far more mature work gradually won its due recognition, not only as a masterpiece to be enjoyed in its own right and for its wonderful music, but as the first invaluable step in Wagner's transformation of opera into music drama.

Above: A page from Wagner's manuscript of The Flying Dutchman, *dated September 13, 1841*

Opposite: Playbill for the première of The Flying Dutchman *at the Court Theatre, Dresden, on January 2, 1843, when the opera proved too gloomy for popular taste*

Variations on a Legend

The origin of the legend of the Flying Dutchman is not known, and the development of its various elements is almost as mysterious as the character himself. The basic story, however, which may well be a relatively modern variation on the theme of the Wandering Jew, was certainly familiar and had been recounted in several European countries before Wagner took it up. In England, for example, it first turned up in printed form as an anonymous short story in the then popular *Blackwood's Magazine* during the year 1821. Though this tale was short, its title was long in the manner of the times: 'Vanderdecken's Message Home: or The Tenacity of Natural Affection.' The narrator of the story is on board an English ship which has just set sail from the Cape of Good Hope. Conversation among the seamen is directed towards the legend of the Flying Dutchman, with which it is assumed that everyone present is familiar. Seventy years earlier, it is recalled, the impulsive Vanderdecken, the skipper of a Dutch ship, had sworn during a heavy storm that he would round Table Bay 'though I should beat here until the Day of Judgment'. Taken at his word, he is still sailing the ocean, always bringing foul weather and misfortune to any ship that sights him. He is dreaded by all other seamen, for it is his custom to hail other ships and ask them, if they are homeward bound, to take over bundles of letters for delivery to his family and friends in Holland. 'No good', adds one of the sailors contributing to the tale, 'ever comes to anyone who communicates with him.'

Not long after this conversation takes place the Flying Dutchman's ship sails close by, and its boat brings one of the crew with the usual letters from the captain. The Dutch sailor becomes angry when the English seamen, having glanced at the letters, tell him that most of the people to whom they are addressed have been dead for many years, Vanderdecken's wife among them. Even though nobody will touch them, he insists on leaving the letters on the deck and then returns to his own ship. Eventually, to the relief of the English crew, the pile of letters is blown into the sea by a sudden gust of wind, and when the weather immediately improves they joyfully declare that it is because they have rid themselves of Vanderdecken's baleful influence. There is no specific mention of the supernatural in this version of the legend, no hint that the Dutchman has made an agreement with Satan, with its attendant escape clause by which he is permitted to land every seven years in search of a woman whose love will save him from the curse. On the contrary, as indicated by the story's sub-title, the author is particularly touched by the 'tenacity of natural affection' which is exemplified by the captain's continuing to write to his wife and friends even after an absence of seventy years.

Below: James Mason and Ava Gardner in a 1951 MGM film, Pandora and the Flying Dutchman, *based on the legend*

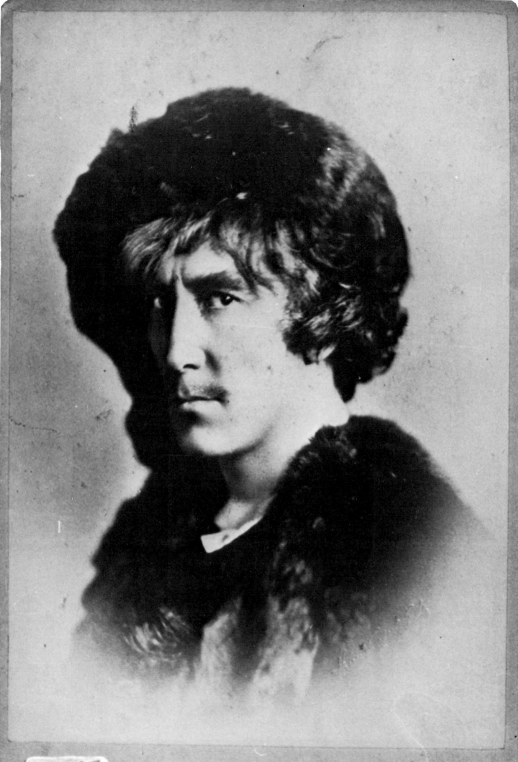

In 1826 an apparently trivial and pedestrian play entitled *The Flying Dutchman, or The Phantom Ship*, a 'nautical drama in three acts', was presented at London's Adelphi Theatre. This was based, its author admitted, on the story in *Blackwood's Magazine*, though his own imaginative additions tended to run contrary to the general conception of the legend and were mercifully ignored by later writers who treated the subject. In *Murder as a Fine Art*, published a year after the play, Thomas De Quincey made a passing reference to the Flying Dutchman when describing the bravery with which the philosopher Descartes was reputed to have saved himself from death at the hands of threatening seamen. De Quincey's casual way of making this reference suggests that he felt sure his readers would be familiar with the legend, but it should be remembered that he was for a time a member of the editorial staff of *Blackwood's Magazine*, for which this particular essay was in fact written, and this might well have influenced him.

The Flying Dutchman seems to have steered a fairly steady course through English literature at this time, because in 1839 there appeared a full-length novel on the theme, *The Phantom Ship*, by Captain Marryat. In this version the name of the Dutch captain again appears as Vanderdecken, though there is still no suggestion of Satan's having a hand in the plot or the victim's being offered any chance of ultimate salvation. It is true that Vanderdecken makes his rash vow to round the Cape come what may, but in doing so he invokes the power of a sacred relic, a fragment of the Cross worn by his wife on her neck. He writes, or rather over-writes, a letter to her describing what had happened: 'The hurricane burst upon the ship, the canvas flew away in ribbons; mountains of sea swept over us, and in the centre of a deep, o'erhanging cloud, which shrouded all in darkness, were written in letters of vivid flame these words— UNTIL THE DAY OF JUDGMENT'. Only if he looks once again on her sacred relic, he concludes, will his present suffering come to an end.

From this point onwards the novel bears no relation whatsoever to the legend as we encounter it elsewhere. Philip, the son of Vanderdecken, sets out with the talisman to find and redeem his father, experiencing several marvellous adventures on the way. He finally reaches Vanderdecken, and in the moment of their reunion the ship breaks up. As father and son

Opposite: Henry Irving in Vanderdecken, *the play by W. G. Wills and Percy Fitzgerald produced at the Lyceum Theatre in 1878*

sink beneath the waves, 'all nature smiled as if it rejoiced that a charm was dissolved for ever, and that THE PHANTOM SHIP WAS NO MORE'. (The good Captain Marryat was the kind of rip-roaring storyteller who is always liable to break out in capital letters.) The novel also introduces a sinister character named Schriften, the ship's pilot whom Vanderdecken had knocked overboard at the Cape. Like the Dutchman himself, Schriften is destined to live for ever, his mission being to lead Philip to destruction and so prevent his taking the holy relic to his father, though at the end he also is released from his fate by the young man's magnanimity.

Wagner made no use of Marryat's version of the legend either in the final poem he wrote for his own music drama or for the original scenario which he sold in 1841 to Léon Pillet of the Paris Opéra, who passed the material on to two hack librettists for re-shaping. Their ramshackle text, which Pierre Dietsch set to music with conspicuous lack of success, changed Vanderdecken into a Norwegian with the name of Troil. It is interesting

Left to right: Engravings from the Illustrierte Zeitung of October 7, 1843, show the original cast: Wilhelmine Schröder-Devrient as Senta, Karl Risse as Daland, Reinhold as Erik, Frau Wächter as Mary and Johann Michael Wächter as the Dutchman

that the French librettists also made Troil guilty of having killed his pilot, which suggests that one of them at least must have been familiar with Marryat's novel. This theory is given additional support by the fact that they gave their opera the title of *Le vaisseau fantôme*.

The version of the legend which seems to have influenced Wagner most profoundly is the one which appears in Heinrich Heine's *Memoirs of Herr von Schnabelewopski*. This fictitious gentleman recalls a play he once saw in Amsterdam on the subject of the Flying Dutchman. He recounts the action of the play in mocking vein, commenting on the Dutchman's failure to redeem himself through a faithful woman: 'Time after time he is glad enough to be saved from marriage, so back he goes to his ship.' Heine describes the drama up to the moment when the Dutchman encounters Katharina, the daughter of a Scots sea captain, but then his Schnabelewopski meets a pretty girl in the audience, takes her away from the theatre to enjoy an hour's sexual pleasure, and returns just in time to catch the final scene.

Although the Dutchman has warned her of the dangers she would run if she decides to share her life with him, Katharina throws herself into the sea in the wake of his departing ship, which immediately sinks. The fascinating point here is that Heine does not treat the supposed play seriously, let alone tragically. He had himself written tragedies at the beginning of his literary career, but soon tired of the form, and though in later life he wrote a considerable amount of fine lyric poetry, he found satire the most congenial medium of all. His prose works, constituting journalism of the highest order, gave him an outlet for his wit and cynicism, and it was these qualities, together with his intellectual agility, which appealed especially to the cultured circle of Paris, where he spent the last twenty-five years of his life. It is not so surprising, therefore, that Heine's final judgment on the Amsterdam play was that it provides two morals: first, that girls should take care not to marry Flying Dutchmen, and secondly, that men may come to grief through even the best of women.

In spite of its cynical conclusion, however, Heine's story did introduce one vital new element into the legend—the idea of man's redemption by woman. Even though he seems to have set up this moral motive only to destroy it with malicious laughter, Heine certainly gave to the legend the spiritual kernel which made it such an irresistible subject for Wagner. It is surely not without significance that the composer was subsequently to refer to Senta's ballad, in which she sees herself as the Dutchman's redeemer, as the musical kernel of the whole work, from which the rest of the music would naturally develop. Wagner must have known the legend itself, which every writer of stories about the Flying Dutchman freely admitted was common knowledge, but the redemption motive came from Heine. When he came to write his autobiography more than twenty years after the conception and composition of *The Flying Dutchman*, Wagner pointedly omitted to acknowledge the fact. It has been suggested, as a result of this, that perhaps Heine had not in fact invented the redemption motive after all, and that Wagner had subsequently learned its true origin. It is more likely, however, that the composer's omission of his indebtedness to Heine is just another example of his rejection of one-time friends and benefactors.

There is yet another story of a phantom ship which Wagner

Opposite: A painting of 1870 showing Senta about to throw herself from the cliffs to prove her fidelity

might have read, and although it did not influence his own poem in any way it deserves a mention if only to demonstrate how extensively this basic legend had fired the imaginations of English and German writers of the early decades of the nineteenth century. Wilhelm Hauff, an unusually promising poet and novelist who died at the age of twenty-five, devised a novel called *Die Karawane* which might be said to have crossed Chaucer's *Canterbury Tales* with the *Arabian Nights' Entertainments*. The members of an Oriental caravan pass the time on their journey by recounting adventures in their own lives, and one of them tells the story of 'The Phantom Ship'. His own vessel had been wrecked one night after sighting a ghostly ship, which he and his old servant, the only survivors, subsequently boarded. They find the corpses of the crew on blood-stained decks, and the captain nailed through his head to the mast. Every night, however, skipper and crew come to life to man the ship, until finally the storyteller and his servant secure the help of a magician to take the crew on land for burial. The captain revives for sufficient time to explain what has happened. Many years ago he was a pirate who killed a holy man, whose dying curse was that he and his crew should live only during the night and die with each dawn until their bodies were buried. Unable ever to reach land by their own efforts, they had tried vainly to wreck their ship on some dangerous cliff, just as Wagner's Dutchman tried to destroy himself.

All these stories based on the legend of a doomed sea captain differ in their details, but the essential element remains constant throughout all the variations. It was therefore a part of European folk-lore. The dramatic astuteness of Wagner was to seize on this myth which would be familiar to his audience, incorporate into it the one valuable new feature supplied by Heine, and transform the whole into a poetic text so designed that it would both fire his musical inspiration and suit the new style of composition upon which he was about to embark. His poem achieved both these objectives with conspicuous success, even though it lacked the profundity and subtlety of his later masterpieces. What is more, he made the legend his own. Heine, Marryat and others had treated it earlier in their individual ways, but their versions are remembered today only in so far as they help us to understand how Wagner arrived at *his* conception of it. The Flying Dutchman has become in-

dissolubly associated with Wagner, and with him alone.

Wagner, it might be added, felt that he had a personal affinity with the Flying Dutchman. He had been a wanderer for most of his adult life, unable to return to his homeland because of his debts, and he had quickly come to detest Paris, where he felt a rootless stranger. His marriage to Minna was never a complete success, for although she did much to comfort him and care for his material needs she never understood his sense of mission in the slightest degree. Like his operatic hero, he craved for a blindly loyal, self-sacrificing woman. 'It was the longing of my Flying Dutchman', he wrote later, 'for *the woman*, not the wife who waited for Odysseus but the redeeming Woman whose character I could not see in any definite form but who was only dimly present in my imagination as the element of Womanhood in principle . . . let me say it in one word, the Woman of the Future.' It is hardly surprising, therefore, that he changed his heroine's name from Minna to Senta.

Below: An engraving done in 1843 showing Senta in mid-flight with the ghost ship already sinking into the sea

Only in legend could Wagner find such a heroine. Even Leonore, the ideal woman of his god-like Beethoven, failed to match his vision, so an opera in the style of *Fidelio* could not satisfy his artistic need. There are parallels, of course, between *Fidelio* and *The Flying Dutchman*, which Irving Singer touches on in his book *Mozart and Beethoven: the Concept of Love in Their Operas*. This writer suggests that 'when Senta accepts the role [of redeemer] she clothes herself in the hard masculinity of the Ballad much as Leonore takes on male attire.' He also points out that the relationship between Erik, Wagner's only major addition to the legend, and Senta duplicates the relationship between Jaquino and Marzelline in *Fidelio*, while Daland shares the mundane, bourgeois characteristics of Rocco. The basic difference between Beethoven and Wagner is that while the former could resolve the drama through his faith in human goodness and God's grace, the latter believed in neither and had to find a solution in myth and a certain mysticism.

Synopsis of the Plot

Set in Norway during the eighteenth century, the opera is in three acts. Although it is the custom of most opera houses to present the acts separately, providing intervals for the social convenience of their patrons and the greater profits of their bars, it was Wagner's wish that they should be performed without a break. This is dramatically sensible since the action is virtually continuous and takes place within a period of twenty-four hours.

Act I: A steep, rocky shore on the Norwegian coast. The cliffs in the foreground form gorges on either side from which echoes can be heard from time to time. A violent storm lashes the waves on the open sea in the background, but there is relative calm between the rocks. A Norwegian ship lies at anchor close to the shore, where it has been driven to take refuge from the storm even though it has almost reached home. On board the sailors are occupied with their duties, furling sails and coiling ropes, while Daland, their captain, has come ashore to ascertain their position.

He descends from his vantage point of the cliff, realising that they are only seven miles from harbour and lamenting the misfortune that has delayed their arrival. His exasperation is increased by his being able to glimpse his home, where his daughter Senta is awaiting his return. Complaining that the wind is no more to be trusted than Satan himself, he goes aboard his ship to send his crew below deck to rest, leaving the helmsman to keep watch for the night. The latter, as tired as everyone else, tries to keep awake by singing a song to the girl of his fancy, but finally sleep overcomes his sense of duty. As the sky grows darker and the storm breaks out again, a ship with black masts and blood-red sails makes for the shore on the opposite side to Daland's ship, casting anchor with a crash which causes the helmsman to wake up, though only momentarily. It is the Flying Dutchman, whose crew begin the

Opposite: Title-page of an album of melodies from the opera arranged for the piano by Fritz Spindler

Stücke aus der Oper

Der fliegende Holländer

von

R. WAGNER

für Piano frei übertragen

von

FRITZ SPINDLER.

Werk 122.

Eigenthum der Verleger. Eingetragen in das Vereins Archiv

BERLIN,
C. F. MESER.
(Adolph Fürstner)

Königl. Sächs. Hof-Musikalienhandlung

Den Verträgen gemäfs deponirt.

Arrangement für das Pianoforte à 4 ms.

von

Theodor Herbert.

LONDON, SCHOTT & C°

Right: Sir Charles
Santley appeared as the
Dutchman in the first
London production of
the opera, at Drury
Lane in 1870, when it
was sung in Italian as
L'Olandese dannato

task of furling sail in an uncanny silence.

The Dutchman himself comes ashore, a sinister figure
wearing black clothes in Spanish style. Seven years, he
soliloquises, have passed since he last stepped on dry land, so
once again he can make a bid for redemption from his fate. He
fears that his torment will never come to an end, that his only

*Left: Emma
Albani sang Senta in
the first Covent
Garden production
(1877), also given in
Italian but this time as
Il Vascello fantasma*

way of release is a hopeless quest. He recalls the curse which
condemns him to sail the oceans for all eternity and his efforts to
overcome it by driving his ship on to dangerous rocks and even
by tempting pirates to take the treasure-laden vessel. However
desperately he seeks death, it seems he is fated to survive,
longing for the Day of Judgment itself. His final cry for

Right: Anton van Rooy, the Dutch bass-baritone who became a famous Dutchman

perpetual extinction is repeated by the unseen crew below deck. As he leans exhausted against a rock Daland comes out of his cabin and, seeing the strange ship at anchor close by, reprimands the helmsman for falling asleep at his post.

Daland now catches sight of the Dutchman, whom he greets and questions as to his name and country. The stranger replies only that he is a Dutchman, without revealing his name, but goes on to intrigue Daland by relating how he has sailed for more years than he cares to remember without being able to find his homeland. He ends by asking Daland to take him into his home for a time, making it clear that he has sufficient treasure to repay handsomely any hospitality that is afforded him. The Norwegian captain agrees at once, shrewdly requesting a sight of the treasure. At a signal from the Dutchman some of his seamen bring ashore a large chest, which is opened to reveal a store of precious stones. As he gazes on it Daland wonders aloud who could be rich enough to offer a price for it. The stranger promptly replies that he will offer the whole of it for a night's shelter, and goes on to ask if Daland has a daughter. He himself has neither wife nor child.

The moment Daland gives an affirmative answer the Dutchman cries out 'Let her be my wife!' Daland expresses complete amazement, yet he makes it clear at once that the thought of securing so much wealth is an irresistible temptation. 'I am almost afraid to hesitate,' he murmurs to himself, 'in case he changes his mind.' Aloud, he repeats that he indeed has a daughter, a beautiful and virtuous girl who is his pride and comfort and who is truly devoted to him. The Dutchman is overjoyed by what Daland tells him: a daughter who is so true to her father will become just as true to her husband. Having piously observed that a faithful wife is the most precious jewel of all, Daland tells the Dutchman that he is so moved by his misfortunes and impressed by his generous nature that he will gladly accept him as his son-in-law, adding somewhat unconvincingly that he would do so even if his fortune were far less. Having made their agreement the two men separately express their satisfaction: the one at securing a rich son-in-law, the other at having finally found the 'angel' who will save him. Then, the storm suddenly subsiding, they make practical arrangements. Daland suggests they sail their ships home together, but the Dutchman insists that he should go on ahead to greet his waiting daughter. His own crew, he explains, are still tired and need a little more rest. Also, since his ship is fast, he will soon catch up. Daland boards his own ship, pipes the crew, and sails off in high spirits.

Act II: A large room in Daland's house. Charts and sea-pictures hang on all the walls, the most prominent being a portrait of a pale man with a dark beard who is dressed in Spanish style. Senta, Daland's daughter, leans back in a high chair, her eyes fixed on this portrait, so absorbed in her dreams that she is unaware of the bustle around her. A number of girls, seated around the fireplace, are spinning under the supervision of Mary, Senta's old nurse. As they work they sing merrily about their lovers at sea, vowing that if their spinning wheels were the wind the ship would bring them back more quickly. They hope the sailors will come home with plenty of gold, which will become their reward for spinning well.

Mary chides Senta for her idleness, saying that she does not deserve any lover's gift. The girls teasingly comment that Senta has no need to worry: her lover, Erik, is not a sailor returning home with gifts only from time to time, but a hunter who brings a daily supply of game. Senta pays no heed to their chatter, remaining in silent contemplation of the portrait. Mary rebukes her again, this time for dreaming her life away on the mere picture of a man, to which Senta responds by asking her why she told her about him in the first place. She expresses her pity for him, which makes the other girls tease her all the more: Erik will become jealous of the man in the picture and shoot his rival off the wall. Now Senta grows angry and tells them to stop their stupid song, which they counter by asking her to sing something herself. To the annoyance of Mary she offers to sing the ballad of the Flying Dutchman, and when she bids the girls pay attention to the words so that they might learn to pity the man as much as she does, all except Mary stop their work to listen.

The ballad concerns the pallid man of the portrait, the master of a ship with black mast and blood-red sails, who keeps unceasing watch from the deck. He sails the world without aim or peace, knowing that his voyage can only end if he succeeds in finding a woman who will be faithful to him to the point of death itself. He is cursed in this fashion because one day he tried to round a dangerous cape in a raging storm, crying out in a desperate moment: 'I will never give up until Judgment Day itself!' His words were overheard by Satan, who condemned him to do exactly as he had sworn. Once in every seven years, however, the Flying Dutchman is allowed to land in search of the 'angel of redemption' who will save him from this terrible fate. This chance has come many times, but he has never found a

Left: George London as the Dutchman at the Metropolitan Opera, New York

woman prepared to be faithful to him and has accordingly been driven back to sea. The ballad so moves the other girls that they first join in with Senta, then continue with it after she falls back exhausted in her chair. Who, they ask, will finally save the Dutchman? At this, Senta stands up in an ecstasy of emotion and cries out that if God will send the Dutchman to her, *she* will save him.

Erik enters just in time to hear this rash promise, for he has been told of Daland's imminent arrival and has come to give Senta the news. The girls, after some argument with Mary, rush out to meet the returning sailors, leaving Senta and Erik alone. She wishes to follow the others, but he holds her back to listen

Right: Cornell MacNeil as the Dutchman at the Metropolitan Opera, New York

to his final plea. Daland, he tells her, is determined to find a husband for her before he goes to sea again. He himself is in love with her, though he is afraid that Daland will not think a hunter good enough to marry his daughter. He is clearly asking Senta to declare that she returns his love and will seek her father's consent to their marriage. To his despair, however, Senta refuses to listen to him, saying that she must go at once to welcome Daland. Although she tries to reassure him at first, he remains convinced that Daland thinks only of wealth and is looking for a richer son-in-law than *he* would make.

He then turns to reproaching her for being indifferent towards him and for having become obsessed by the man whose portrait hangs on the wall. When she confesses that she is deeply moved by the thought of the man's unhappy fate Erik begs her to consider his own suffering, only to provoke her to reply scornfully that there can be no comparison. The plight of the Flying Dutchman is a permanent wound in her heart. Erik, crying out that she has been ensnared by Satan, decides to tell her of a dream he had, a dream which he believes was sent as a warning to them both. He saw her father arrive on shore with a stranger, a man exactly resembling the portrait. Next he saw her run from the house to greet her father, but fall down before the stranger instead, clasping his knees. Senta, who seems to have been sharing Erik's vision, joins in his story, imagining the stranger raising her to her feet. Erik rushes away in horror as she exclaims: 'He is looking for me, and I shall find him and die with him!' As she prays that her dream will come true the door opens to admit Daland and the Dutchman.

Senta remains motionless as the two men enter, giving a startled cry when her eyes leave the portrait to look straight at the face of the Dutchman, who has walked forward to meet her. Daland, finding himself left behind in the doorway, gently reproves her for failing to greet him with her usual ready kiss and embrace. Even when she does take his hand, her first question is about the stranger. Daland replies that he is a seaman like himself, but one banished from his homeland who seeks their hospitality. He asks her if she will agree to let the stranger stay with them, and when she nods her assent he turns to the Dutchman. Is not this daughter everything he claimed she was? Addressing Senta again, he bids her treat their guest with friendship, then in the next breath bids her to take him as her husband. Senta remains spellbound, taking no notice of the jewels which Daland shows her. She and the Dutchman have eyes only for each other, so that Daland realises his presence is no longer required and walks slowly out of the room.

Left alone, the couple at first express their own individual thoughts, he his wonder at meeting the kind of woman he has dreamed of for so many lonely years, she her amazement that the man whose portrait has dominated her mind for so long is now standing before her. Then the Dutchman speaks directly to Senta, asking her if she is really prepared to accept him as a husband and share his life, bringing him comfort at last. She replies that she will obey her father's wish without question, for

it is her own wish too. When he warns her of the danger in
accepting him as husband, she replies that she knows where her
duty lies, a duty which she holds to be sacred. Destiny, she adds,
may pass judgment on her, but she is only obeying its call.
Conscious of the demands of loyalty, she offers her whole
being to him, swearing in an outburst of ecstasy that she will
remain constant until the moment of death itself. There is no
conventional expression of mutual love in their exchanges,
which pass beyond the realm of natural human passion to that
of a wholly spiritual union of souls, the one prepared to sacrifice
itself to save the other from a supernatural fate.

Daland returns, bringing matters down again to the earthly, material level. He apologises for interrupting them with the excuse that everything has been made ready for the festivities which always take place on his return home from a voyage. In his usual blunt, jovial manner he first asks the Dutchman if he has had time enough to propose to his daughter, then bids Senta tell him what her answer has been. He is delighted, if not surprised by their replies, though he has not the slightest understanding of the true situation. His attitude is simply that of a middle-class father anxious to secure a good match for his daughter, and so much the better if she finds him personally

59

Opposite: Milla Andrew as Senta in the Sadler's Wells production of 1969

attractive. An almost cynical materialist, he sees no further than the Dutchman's enormous wealth, which makes him a worthier son-in-law than he had ever dreamed of finding. Assuring them with unintentional irony that they will never regret their decision, he urges them to the festivities which are already under way.

Act III: An inlet with a rocky shore, showing Daland's house to one side of the foreground, with the two ships lying close to each other in the background. The clear night reveals the contrast between the two ships: the Norwegian crew are noisily celebrating on deck, whereas there is no movement aboard the Dutch vessel. Daland's men call out to the other crew to come and join them in their feasting and dancing, but they receive no reply. The girls who arrive with food and drink from the house also offer hospitality to the sailors on the strange ship, only to meet with the same total lack of response. They grow afraid when their men point out that the ship might be that of the Flying Dutchman, of whom they have all heard uncanny stories, and they leave in some terror when the Norwegian sailors taunt the silent crew, daring them to set their sails and demonstrate the speed of their ghost ship. The men's singing and dancing is interrupted by shouts from the Dutch ship as a sudden violent wind whistles through its rigging.

The ghost crew call on their captain either to show them his promised bride or return to them for another seven years' voyage protected by Satan from any danger the sea can threaten. The Norwegian crew counter this sinister chant with ever noisier singing and dancing, but when this proves to have no effect they are overcome with fright and leave the deck, crossing themselves as they go below. At this the Dutch crew give out a burst of shrill, mocking laughter before falling silent again as at the beginning of the scene.

Senta comes hurrying from the house, followed by an almost hysterical Erik. He can scarcely believe that she has promised to marry a man whom she has known only for a few hours, and when she brusquely replies that she must do it because it is her duty he reminds her that she already had a duty to him. When Senta attempts to deny this the dumbfounded Erik reminds her of the days in the past when he used to risk his neck climbing to gather mountain flowers for her, when Daland would always entrust her to his care while he himself was away at sea, and

60

when she would place her arm around him to assure him of her affection. Was not all this, he demands, proof of her love for him? Before Senta can defend herself the couple are interrupted by the Dutchman, who has observed everything that has passed between them. He rushes forward with a cry that all is lost and he has no option except to go back to sea and take up his hopeless quest once again.

Although Senta bars his path and falls at his feet pleading with him to stay, the Dutchman calls out to his crew to hoist sail and weigh anchor. He tells Senta with bitterness that she has betrayed her word, leaving him with no trust either in her or in God, while Erik cries out that she is in the clutches of Satan. The Dutchman then spells out for Senta the situation at which he has previously only hinted, that any woman who swears to be faithful to him and then breaks that promise is doomed to eternal damnation. He adds sorrowfully that many girls have already suffered this fate, which prompts Erik to call on his friends to save Senta. As the girls come rushing from the house with Daland, and the Norwegian sailors tumble ashore from their ship, the Dutchman assures Senta that at least she will be spared the fate of his other promised brides. She swore to be true to him until death, but she did not invoke the name of God when she made this vow. Then he turns to the whole crowd assembled on the shore, declaring himself to be the Flying Dutchman, the terror of all God-fearing mariners throughout the world. He makes swiftly for the deck of his ship while Daland and Erik restrain Senta from following him.

As the Dutch crew, shouting their ghostly cries, turn their ship from the shore to head out to the open sea, Senta desperately tears herself free. Reaching the edge of a huge rock overhanging the sea, she cries out to the Dutchman: 'Now praise your angel of deliverance, for I shall prove my fidelity.' She leaps into the sea, at which the ship sinks with all hands beneath a huge wave that becomes a whirlpool. In the glow of the setting sun the transfigured forms of Senta and the Dutchman are seen rising towards the heavens, clasped in each other's arms. The almost mystic ideal of man redeemed by the constancy of a woman's love has been completely fulfilled.

Opposite: Gwyneth Jones as Senta in the BBC television production of 1975, in which the customary portrait of the Dutchman was replaced by a statue

Wagner's Advice to the Players

Wagner remains unique among dramatic composers concerning his involvement in every aspect of the presentation of his stage works. He was his own librettist from the very beginning, writing his own text for *Die Feen*, composed during 1833–34 when he was twenty years old but not produced until 1888, based on Carlo Gozzi's comedy *La Donna Serpente*. As he began to develop his idea of opera as a complete synthesis of all the arts, he placed a correspondingly greater emphasis on the importance of the text, which he referred to always as the 'poem' to distinguish it from the kind of competent yet in itself uninspired material turned out in factory-belt fashion by Eugène Scribe and his less commercially successful colleagues. Even then, it was not sufficient for Wagner to be poet as well as composer, because he felt that all his dedicated work in these two capacities would be undermined by unimaginative stage production which either failed to fulfil or, even worse, worked directly against his dramatic and musical intentions.

As creator of the work of art, he held it imperative that he should also supervise its staging and scenic realisation, which in turn meant that he should control the cast's acting just as much as its singing. In pursuit of this ideal he published in 1853, ten years after the opera's première, his *Remarks on Performing the Opera 'The Flying Dutchman'*, an essay from which all producers and singers still have much to learn. It cannot be emphasised too strongly that Wagner was not a mere theorist, but a man with an inborn sense of theatre who could not only tell the singers at rehearsal how to act a particular scene but also demonstrate how to do it in practice. It might even be said that in gaining a great dramatic composer Germany lost a potentially superb actor.

Opposite: Anja Silja, a modern-style Senta in Munich

Although his 'remarks' are directed mainly towards the singers, and the Dutchman himself above all, Wagner begins by reminding conductor and producer that there must always be

64

Right: Ludwig Schnorr von Carolsfeld, seen as Erik in this print by his father Julius, was subsequently to create the role of Tristan in Munich on June 10, 1865, dying only six weeks later at the tragically early age of twenty-nine

SENTA.   ERICK.

18§63   Der fliegende Holländer.   Richard Wagner.

complete accord between what passes in the orchestra and what is shown on the stage. The sea and the two ships, in particular, require meticulous presentation as he has stipulated in the score. He points out that the opening scene has to put the spectator into the right frame of mind to accept the mysterious figure of the Dutchman when he first makes his appearance. This can only be achieved by showing the sea between the headlands as

truly dangerous and frightening during the storm passages, by designing Daland's ship in full naturalistic detail, and by making it visibly heel when struck by a particularly large wave between the two verses of the drowsy helmsman's song. He demands careful attention too to the matter of lighting, so that the audience's imagination will be concentrated on the capricious moods of the elements to which all seamen are

67

exposed. Wagner is not insisting here on a realistic setting for its own sake, or to create an impressive stage picture, but in order to make the spectator aware of the conditions under which seafaring people live and work. It is these conditions, he is implicitly arguing, which cause seamen and their families on land to accept the legend of the Flying Dutchman so readily, even, as in the case of Senta, to become obsessed by it. Having instructed producer and designer what to do, Wagner is content to leave the manner of doing it to their own inventive skills.

His advice to the players is similarly strict yet generalised so far as Senta, Daland and Erik are concerned. He expresses the hope that the role of his heroine will not be found difficult to understand and interpret, but is firm in his warning that the dreamy side to her nature must not be shown in the 'modern' sense of sickly sentimentality. Senta is a robust girl of healthy Northern temperament, the deep compassion she feels for the Dutchman's fate springing from her naïvety. It is her innocence which gives her the strength to sacrifice herself to save him, the same innocence which has made her always obedient to her father.

Wagner is equally insistent that Erik should not be portrayed as a weak and whining creature of sentiment. On the contrary, he is a stormy, impulsive young man, though sombre at times in the manner of a hunter who works alone. His attempts to dissuade Senta from marrying the man her father has chosen for her are not outbursts of petulance but the logical, if sometimes desperately vehement arguments of a realist who can see the danger into which her idealism might lead her. Daland, too, is a strong, down-to-earth character, a seaman who faces tempests and the other hazards of his work to make an honest living. Wagner makes it clear that he should not be played as a stock character of comedy because he appears ready to sell his daughter to a wealthy suitor. A hundred thousand other fathers in any part of Europe would do the same, righteously believing they were doing the best for their daughters. In this casual, parenthetic comment we hear the voice of the revolutionary, rather than that of the artist, sniping with deadly accuracy at the false bourgeois morality he so wholeheartedly despised.

Wagner concentrates ninety per cent of his remarks on the way in which he wants the role of the Dutchman to be acted. It should be noted that it is the acting of the part, not its singing, with which he is concerned, for this is something quite new in the operatic field. All composers have indicated how they wished their music to be sung, and some, like Verdi, have expressed general ideas regarding the physical representation of the characters on the stage. Never before, however, had any composer dealt in such minute detail with this latter aspect of performance and interpretation. Wagner devoted three whole pages to an analysis of the Dutchman's opening monologue, not only stipulating the necessary vocal nuances but describing every stance and gesture he desired the performer to make. The true success of the music drama, as the total work of art he intended it to be, depended on an intelligent and psychologically convincing portrayal of the title-role.

First of all, the singer is requested to adhere strictly to every detail of his outward appearance as specified by the composer in his score. His entry must be solemn and earnest, the deliberate slowness of his walking ashore affording a marked contrast to

Below: The first performance of The Flying Dutchman *in English was given by the Carl Rosa Opera Company at the Lyceum Theatre in London in 1876 with Sir Charles Santley as the Dutchman and Ottavia Torriani as Senta*

his ship's unnaturally rapid passage across the sea and the eagerness with which ordinary seamen leap on to the land they love. He must nevertheless move with the rolling gait characteristic of all sailors, for his landing is accompanied by wavelike figures for the strings, and he is even instructed to time his second step to coincide with the first crotchet of the third bar, his third and fourth with the notes of the eighth and tenth bars. Throughout his entrance he is told to move with sunken head and folded arms. After this his movements will 'follow the dictates of his words', yet however strong the expression of his emotions there must be no exaggerated striding to and fro: the establishment of the Dutchman's essential character calls for a 'terrible repose' in the performer's outward demeanour.

Below : The realistic setting for the opening scene in Bayreuth's first production of The Flying Dutchman, *which was surprisingly delayed until 1901*

Wagner leaves nothing to chance in the narration itself, because he believes it is the most difficult scene for the performer to handle and also the one on which the whole credibility of the character ultimately depends. The first phrases of the recitative, '*Die Frist ist um*' ('The time is up'), are to be sung without a trace of passion, as though the man were completely exhausted, and his angry '*Ha! Stolzer Ozean!*' should be delivered with bitter restraint, the actor merely turning his head a little to look out across the sea. Even when he cries out that his pain will last forever, it is sufficient for him just to bow his head in passive weariness. He should remain still even in swearing he will live out the full extent of his fate, staring blankly before him.

Wagner is prepared to allow the actor to move during the *allegro* section, '*Wie oft in Meeres tiefsten Schlund*' ('How often into the ocean's depths'), but however agonised are the feelings he is expressing his general movements should remain calm, allowing himself only a modest gesture of hand or arm. His lament '*Nirgens ein Grab! Niemals der Tod!*' ('There is no grave nor death!') is only a *description* of his suffering, so it must not be acted out as a physical collapse into despair. During the orchestral postlude to his explanation of the curse laid upon him, the actor is instructed gradually to raise his head to look at the sky, and with the entry of the muffled roll on the kettledrum to clench his down-held fists, continuing this stance through-out the subsequent direct appeal to the angel of God who might yet deliver him. The Dutchman at this point should be seen by the audience as a fallen angel himself. Only when he cries out that hope is a delusion may he allow himself to stand with his whole body erect, finally unleashing his physical energy in full force to declare his longing for the Day of Judgment. The end of the monologue should find the Dutchman standing like a statue, his arms fully raised in defiance, a position he must hold during the *fortissimo* section of the postlude. He relaxes only as the music gradually dies down, and in time to it, so that by the end he is seen as drained of emotion and energy once more, a dejected figure with bowed head and folded arms, leaning against a wall of rock.

This summary of Wagner's detailed instructions to the singer about a monologue lasting slightly less than ten minutes should make clear the importance he attached to acting in his music

Below: Scrupulously detailed setting for Act II at the Berlin Staatsoper in 1910

dramas. He deals similarly with the scene between Daland and the Dutchman in Act I, and with the latter's meeting with Senta in Act II. It is perhaps worth mentioning here one emphatic point which he makes concerning the immobility of actors at certain crucial moments in the drama, because it is one which applies to many of his later works, notably in the scenes where Siegmund and Sieglinde (*Die Walküre*) and Tristan and Isolde

„Der Fliegende Holländer." Akt II, Scene 3.
Daland: „Mein Kind, du siehst mich auf der Schwelle:
Wie? Kein Umarmen? Keinen Kuß?"

face each other and experience the dawning wonder of love. When Daland leaves Senta and the Dutchman alone together, hoping that they will agree to marriage on the mundane terms within his own limited understanding, Wagner insists that the couple stand perfectly still in contemplation of each other. He tells the performers not to be afraid that this will be wearisome to the audience: on the contrary, he asserts that experience has

Below: Astrid Varnay with Hans Hotter in Act II at the Metropolitan Opera, New York, in 1950

Above: Varnay with Set Svanholm (Erik) at the Metropolitan

shown that it is precisely this complete immobility of the characters on stage which most engrosses the audience and most effectively prepares it for the ensuing scene.

History has proved Wagner right on this score. Those moments when Senta and the Dutchman, or Tristan and Isolde, stand motionless on the stage never fail to impress the opera-goer and remain deeply etched in his memory. Simply reading Wagner's advice to his players might give the impression that he belongs to the band of pedants who lecture on drama to university students, but when it is carried out in the theatre in practice it is seen to be stunningly effective. He was always a great theoriser, in politics and philosophy as well as music, and there is no denying that many of the ideas he propounded in his writings contradict one another. It is also true that as a composer he did not always carry out in practice some of the theories which he had argued most strenuously. In the case of his various writings on the art of performance, however, he

consistently practised what he preached, demonstrating to the singers at rehearsals exactly what he wanted them to do on the stage. His thinking on other matters might sometimes be muddled, but when it came to the question of how the characters in his music dramas should be acted everything was crystal clear. He had created these characters in the first place, both as poet and composer, so he knew exactly how their outward appearance and behaviour could be made to reveal their innermost nature and states of mind. His *Remarks on Performing the Opera 'The Flying Dutchman'* prove beyond any possible doubt that his profound dramatic perception was matched by an equally remarkable sense of visual theatre.

Above: Opening scene at the Paris Opéra in 1953

The Music

Before looking at the music of *The Flying Dutchman* in detail it is worth noting that it has been consistently underrated as a whole by Wagner scholars. It is one of those curious ironies in musical history that a work which was rejected in the beginning because it was too far in advance of audiences and critics should later be decried on the grounds of not being advanced enough. In 1843 it was indeed revolutionary in its conception, but from this time onwards the composer carried his new ideas to much greater lengths, culminating in the formidable complexities of *Parsifal*. Musicologists writing a century or more later, having the benefit of hindsight, tend to see *The Flying Dutchman* as perfectly straightforward, almost conventional, by comparison. There is a good deal of truth in this when Wagner's work is being regarded in its totality, but the comparison itself is dangerous because it can lead to serious misunderstanding.

Ernest Newman, the most distinguished of all Wagnerian authorities, is not above falling into the trap. When referring to the duet for Daland and the Dutchman in Act I, for example, he first accuses Wagner of occasionally slipping into 'the routine commonplaces of the opera of the epoch' and then suggests that he would have done better to dispense almost entirely with the former character. Parts of this lengthy scene between the two men are certainly cast in formal patterns, but the music is anything but 'commonplace'. Daland is in fact essential to Wagner's total conception, because his very ordinariness throws the Dutchman's supernaturally tortured character into even greater relief, and the fact that he should have a daughter so spiritually perceptive as Senta adds an ironic dimension to the drama. Jack Stein, in his study of Wagner's gradual achievement of a complete synthesis of the arts, is similarly dismissive of Erik's dream narrative in Act II, which he finds 'barren'. Again, however, it is clear that Wagner knew perfectly well what he was doing. A thoroughly normal young man, Erik

Opposite: Leonie Rysanek with Franz Crass at La Scala, Milan, 1965

imagines the sinister stranger's arrival in a completely different way from Senta, so it is psychologically vital that his music should be in a contrasting style to that of her Ballad.

The score of *The Flying Dutchman* admittedly contains the arias, duets and terzettos which the Beethoven of Wagner's imaginative short story appears to scorn. Most of them, however, like the Dutchman's monologue in Act I and Senta's ballad in Act II, are conceived in a new style designed to increase their psychological aptness, while the two or three more conventional numbers are deliberately fashioned to emphasise the gulf separating Senta and the Dutchman on the one hand from Daland and Erik on the other. The word 'numbers' implies that Wagner had not yet freed himself from the past, and *The Flying Dutchman* is in fact a hybrid work, part

Right: Josef Greindl (Daland, centre) with Birgit Nilsson and Tomislav Neralic at the Lyric Opera of Chicago in 1959

opera and part music drama. Even in so mature a work as *Die Meistersinger*, however, there are set numbers such as the Prize Song and the Quintet. What is important in *The Flying Dutchman* is that these more traditional-style arias have a purpose: the conventional person is seen to be conventional by virtue of the music through which he expresses himself. Most of the criticism levelled against the work is not really valid: it is a masterpiece on its own terms, disappointing only to those who confuse the issue by judging it by the criteria of *Tristan und Isolde* or *Parsifal*, works belonging to completely different genres.

Opposite: Franz Crass as the Dutchman at La Scala, Milan, 1965

The true stature and the revolutionary nature of *The Flying Dutchman* is immediately established by the overture, the ending of which was modified in 1851 when Wagner conducted four memorable performances at Zurich during his period of exile in Switzerland. (At the same time he toned down the over-exuberance of his original orchestration.) Hitherto the operatic overture had taken a number of guises. It was in some cases a piece of abstract music in sonata form, in others a haphazard *pot-pourri* of melodies from the opera itself. Most composers had made no genuine effort to relate the overture to the opera at all, so that Rossini, for example, blithely prefaced *The Barber of Seville* with a piece he had already used for two other operas. There are a few earlier examples of composers taking care that the music of the overture should bear some significant relation to the work as a whole, notably Mozart with *The Magic Flute*, but in the case of *The Flying Dutchman* Wagner created something infinitely more far-reaching.

The overture in general is a superb sea-picture in music, so potent that one conductor paid it the back-handed compliment of complaining that 'the wind blows out at you wherever you open the score'. More important, however, is the fact that of the dozen different short melodies, or 'motives', out of which it is constructed, no fewer than nine re-appear during the course of the drama itself. Five of these, all easily identifiable, assume such importance that Newman gave each a convenient name. Against a strident chord the horns and bassoons launch immediately into a stark, unforgettably dramatic motive representing the Dutchman himself, a motive which bears an uncanny resemblance to the first subject of Beethoven's Ninth Symphony, which Wagner himself described as 'bare and mighty'. After this there come exciting passages suggesting the tempest tearing through the rigging and the angry growl of the sea, followed by a return of the Dutchman motive and a succession of calls representing the forces of the ocean.

The doomed captain's Wanderer motive also appears in this first section, which maintains a hectic *allegro con brio* until the music gradually softens down to *andante* for the Redemption motive, introduced by the plaintive voice of the cor anglais. Senta's theme is not fully rounded off here, but fades into the brief yet effective Fate motive. The music then blows up into another stormy section into which is woven the last of the important motives, Longing for Death. The mood changes for a snatch of melody which will eventually be extended into the jolly song of the Norwegian crew, after which the turbulent sea-picture is resumed, dominated by the various motives of Senta

Below: Josef Greindl and Gladys Kuchta in the Deutsche Oper Berlin production, 1965

and the Dutchman. The final section of the overture develops the Redemption motive, presenting it now with the ardent phrases which conclude Senta's ballad, and comes to a close with a transfigured version of the motive indicating a resolution of all the conflict that has passed before.

When the curtain rises on the rocky shore where the Norwegian ship has taken refuge, the orchestral storm is still raging, bringing back themes associated with sea and wind in the overture. The busy sailors contribute a few cries of 'Hojohe!' and 'Hallojo' simply to signal a human presence on the scene. Daland is permitted no more than a few lines of recitative in which to declare that he has discovered their location, only a short distance from home, indulging however in one brief passage of melting lyricism as he thinks of his daughter waiting there for him. The storm having subsided, and the remainder of the crew gone below deck, the Helmsman left on watch is given the first set piece, an engagingly simple song which ideally expresses his yearning to see his girl friend again. It has sufficient melodic appeal to warrant a second verse: Wagner adds a neat dramatic touch by separating it from the first by a snatch of the sailors' chorus to be heard later on. The song is further removed from the commonplace by the arrival of the ghost ship, to eerie music based on the Dutchman motive, and by the Helmsman's momentary awakening to sing the first line of his song before falling asleep again. (By curious coincidence, Verdi's Duke of Mantua, having sung his two-verse '*La donna è mobile*' in the last act of *Rigoletto*, also falls asleep while trying to sing a third verse.)

The Dutchman's opening monologue is one of the glories of the work, a superb example of musico-dramatic writing. As his crew furl sails in ominous silence, he steps ashore to the Fate motive followed by a hesitant phrase played by violas and cellos which symbolises his weariness of life and which returns several times in his recitative. This first section of the Dutchman's self-portrait is skilfully varied in pace, dynamics and instrumental texture, though his first words, '*Die Frist ist um*' ('The time has come'), are intoned on a single note without accompaniment. Voice and orchestra remain subdued until he cries out directly to the ocean, which will soon see him again, resuming a tone of resignation as he reflects that he will never find the grace he needs to save himself. A flurry of rising notes in cellos and basses lead to a sudden energetic declaration that he will always obey the power of the tides, but the music dies down quickly again with his despairing thought that this obedience must endure until the end of time.

The aria '*Wie oft in Meeres tiefsten Schlund*' ('How often into the ocean's depths') opens with an almost swaggering *allegro* over the Wanderer motive in the strings, the singer's first phrase quite new, the second now familiar as the Longing for Death motive. The music here has an exhilaratingly broad sweep, rising to a defiant outburst as the Dutchman recalls how he once challenged pirates to take his ship. To a turbulent outburst in the orchestra he laments that death has always thwarted his attempts at self-destruction. A slow *maestoso* follows, expressing overwhelming grief, as his thoughts turn to heaven and the hope that one day his 'angel of redemption' will be found. Tremolando chords for cellos and basses add to the *frisson* produced by this heartfelt plea, which mounts in eloquence to end *fortissimo*. There is no break here, however, a dozen orchestral bars appropriately marked *feroce* leading straight into the final section of the aria (*molto passionato*), a broad-spanning melody starting with the words '*Nur eine Hoffnung*' in which the doomed man sees release only when the world itself will end, his final plea for annihilation being echoed by the unseen crew of his ship in the hollow tones of a prayer for the dead.

The complexity of the vocal writing of this narration is matched by the intricate contribution of the orchestra, which weaves a variety of motives together in a manner never encountered in any previous dramatic work, resulting in an extension of the power of music to express the psychology as well as the emotion inherent in the situation. That Wagner realised the new dramatic demands he was placing on the singer in the process is clear from the minutely detailed instructions for the performance of the narration which he issued some years later (*see* previous chapter). After the concentrated intensity of the Dutchman's self-portrait it is almost with relief that one welcomes the return of the blunt and genial Daland and the more loosely constructed scene between the two sea captains. Even here, however, *pace* Ernest Newman, the music keeps the drama moving forward as it establishes what is, in the context of opera, a minimal amount of plot.

The realities of ordinary life are restored as Daland angrily

wakes the Helmsman, who makes another drowsy attempt at
his love song, and even when their call to the strange ship does
not produce the expected answer the music retains its hearty,
open-air quality. Daland opens his scene with the Dutchman
with recitative in conventional style, but the latter's replies,
underlined in the orchestra several times by a gloomy melodic
figure for violas and cellos in octaves, are strongly characterful,
leading naturally into a reflective arioso in which he describes
the endless voyaging which keeps him from his home. Whereas
Daland's music might have been written by other composers of
the time, the Dutchman's is unmistakably Wagnerian. There is a
brief lapse into the routine during the conversation about the
treasure unloaded from the ghost ship, which leads to the
Dutchman's offer to give it all in exchange for Senta's hand in
marriage.

85

Above: Milla Andrew singing Senta's Ballad at Sadler's Wells, 1969

Opposite: Gwyneth Jones singing Senta's Ballad at Covent Garden, 1966

The duet starts *allegro giusto*, featuring a swaying melody which is something of a throw-back in style yet which is good enough of its kind. The voices then separate to allow the two men to reach agreement on the bargain, after which the duet is taken up again *allegro agitato* so that each can express his individual joy over the reward it may bring. The Dutchman wonders whether he is at last to find redemption through Senta's love and loyalty, while Daland offers thanks to the storm which has given him this chance meeting with a potential wealthy son-in-law. The music is frankly Italianate in the lilt and graceful charm of its tunes, reminding us of Wagner's youthful admiration for Bellini. There is also a vigorous swing to the music which gives it a kinship to the kind of duet Verdi composed for men vowing eternal friendship, though here the two characters are voicing radically different sentiments. The all-important motives are temporarily forgotten, and it is no doubt for this reason that criticism has been levelled against the duet. Judged on its own merits it constitutes a splendid dramatic scene, carrying the action forward and revealing important facets of the two men's personalities in music that is memorably melodic and fired by true passion.

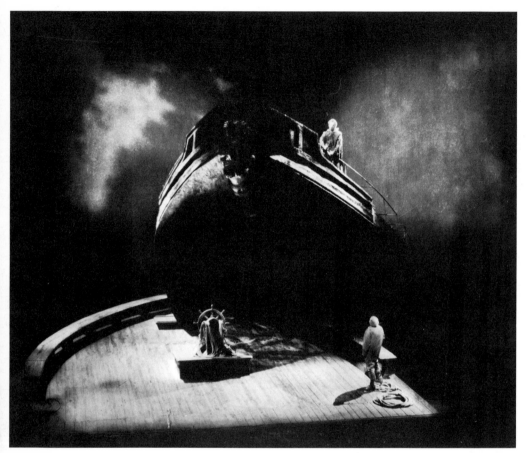

*Above and opposite:
Impressive scenes from
Acts I and III,
produced by August
Everding in settings by
Josef Svoboda at
Bayreuth*

Although the duet reaches a musically formal end, Wagner
makes it appear to be interrupted by the Helmsman's shout that
a south wind has sprung up. The Norwegian crew greet with
their characteristic calls this wind which will carry them home,
and Daland expresses his own pleasure to the lively dance-tune
of the sailors, suggesting he and the Dutchman both set sail at
once. The Dutchman's preference to follow him after his own
crew have rested a little longer is a curious twist of the story,
untypical of Wagner in that it serves no dramatic or musical
purpose. (Newman lets his sense of wit carry him astray on this
point, suggesting that 'The Dutchman's real reason for
postponing his own sailing is of course a matter less of
humanitarianism than of practical operatics. Were Daland and
the Dutchman to reach land again at the same time, Wagner
would lose the opportunity for one of the most impressive

moments of the opera—the Dutchman's unexpected entry into the spinning scene of the second act.' But this is precisely what *does* happen, the two men entering the room at the same moment, to Senta's astonishment.) Daland boards his ship and gives the crew the order to cast loose, which they carry out to a vigorous version of the Helmsman's song. The act concludes with the orchestra recalling several of the now familiar themes associated with the sea.

In the three-act version of *The Flying Dutchman* usually presented in the opera house, the orchestral introduction to Act II begins with a repetition of these same themes, a course imposed on Wagner simply to meet the theatre's demand for the customary intervals. His original intention had been for the work to be given in one continuous act, which was finally carried out at Bayreuth in 1901, when it was realised that the

89

only requirement was a simple cut from the twenty-sixth bar before the end of the postlude of Act I to the nineteenth bar of the prelude to Act II. The sense of continuity is strengthened by the use of a short motive from the sailors' calls as the basic pulse of the main phrase of the Spinning Chorus which opens the second act. This descriptive chorus, in which the orchestral strings suggest the humming of the wheels, is a relatively conventional set-piece, but so irresistibly melodious that it quickly became popular all over Germany. (A brilliant piano transcription was made in 1860 by Liszt, Wagner's future father-in-law.) Its dramatic purpose is to establish an atmosphere of peaceful domesticity after all the tumult and danger of the seafaring life depicted in the previous scene. The girls' thoughts are with their absent lovers, whom they expect back from sea at any moment, and eventually they break off to tease Senta, who sits in silent contemplation of the Dutchman's portrait on the wall, because *her* lover is a landsman. Although she remains silent, her thoughts are revealed by the Redemption motive played in the orchestra.

The ballad which Senta finally sings after further taunting is the very heart of the work's whole conception, and appropriately it occurs exactly mid-point in the score. It was the first number Wagner composed, and in later years he declared that after he had written it he had unconsciously created a thematic kernel whose ideas then spread themselves with inevitable logic through the rest of the music. In the literal sense this was not strictly accurate, since there are many themes in the score which do not feature in the ballad, but the vital Dutchman and Redemption motives are present, as are others relating to the spirit of the sea. The ballad is of course the story of the Dutchman's boastful vow, the curse it brings upon his head, and then in the third stanza the opportunity given to him every seven years to redeem himself. The music is noble and heroic, prefaced by calls of 'Jo-ho-hoe! Jo-ho-ho-hoe!' to the Dutchman motive. The opening melody has a striding rhythm and a strong sweep of phrase, its answering theme a more insinuating character. After the third stanza, when Senta sinks back momentarily exhausted with emotion, the other girls, deeply affected by her narrative, repeat a few bars of the music in gentle tones. Then, in an ecstatic outburst, she declares her own willingness to save the Dutchman from his fate, singing

Opposite: Anja Silja with Thomas Stewart in Wieland Wagner's production at Bayreuth

Overleaf: Jean-Pierre Ponnelle's production at the San Francisco Opera in 1975

Opposite: Rehearsing the Norwegian sailors' dance at Bayreuth

the Redemption motive in its most rapturous form.

Erik appears at this point to announce Daland's arrival, and overhears her final words. His scene with her is delayed for a couple of minutes, however, by the weakest stretch in the score, an undistinguished chattering chorus of the girls who are excited by the return of the menfolk. He sings the first verse of an ardently pleading aria, '*Mein Herz vol Treue bis zum Sterben*', whose graceful line bears witness to the warmth and sincerity of the love he offers. It is a song typical of any vulnerable young suitor, giving no particular insight into Erik's character, yet its mellifluous refinement is quite admirable. Before the second verse of the aria, Senta's attempt to leave him to greet her father is carried on in an exchange of heightened recitative with telling orchestral accompaniment. Wagner's new style of recitative is revealed in its full mastery after the repeat of Erik's song, when Senta scornfully rejects any comparison between his own suffering over her coolness towards him and the infinitely greater torment of the man in the portrait. Here the melodic line is moulded to the accents of the verse so perfectly that the musical emphasis always coincides with the important syllable of the words. Music and poem become as one.

Erik's narration of his dream, which he regards as a direct warning to them both of an impending tragedy, is composed in a highly individual manner which Wagner was subsequently to develop through *Tannhäuser* and *Lohengrin* to *Tristan und Isolde*. Dramatically it is effective in creating a sense of expectancy, hinting to the audience that the dream will shortly become a reality, while the music vividly establishes Erik's trance-like state of mind. When he describes the appearance of the stranger the Dutchman motive steals in menacingly on bassoons and cellos against a background of tremolando violas, producing a truly spine-chilling effect. The duet is crowned by Senta's rapturous cry that the man of her dreams is coming to her at last, and she swears to bind her fate to his. As Erik rushes out of the room in despair Senta sings the Redemption motive in a soft, rapt tone, her gaze fixed to the portrait, ending with a startled scream as she suddenly turns to see the Dutchman standing with Daland in the doorway.

For a time no one speaks, throbbing timpani followed by a striking little figure for the strings in parallel thirds sustaining

the necessary tension. This is eventually broken by Daland's gentle chiding of Senta for not offering him her usual greeting, to which her only reply is to ask the identity of the stranger. Daland replies by way of an aria bouncing with good-natured melody, again in conventional Italianate style complete with an unabashed cadential flourish at one point. Again, however, it should be emphasised that this aria, as well as being tunefully engaging in itself and appropriate to the character for whom it is designed, is a part of the composer's general plan, lowering the tension for a time in readiness for the next tightening of the dramatic screw. It is a device, incidentally, which Shakespeare was fond of using, so it is worth recalling that the Beethoven of Wagner's story declared he would go to work on a musical drama 'as Shakespeare did when he wrote his plays'. Senta and the Dutchman meanwhile, clearly impervious to the charms of bel canto, have remained in silent contemplation of each other. The spiritual nature of their communion is quite beyond the understanding of Daland, who decides to leave them to plan a wedding for the next day.

Even when they are alone at last, the couple can still find no words to say, leaving the orchestra to fill in the silence with recollections of their two distinctive motives. There is no accompaniment, on the other hand, to the Dutchman's opening line of heartfelt recitative leading up to the broad first cantilena of their duet, a melody filled with infinite yearning and one of Wagner's finest inspirations. Senta first enters *mezza voce*, as though musing to herself, but then takes the lead when the two voices combine to give expression to feelings of a love too profound for the brightly rapturous music traditionally provided at such a moment. Wagner finds the ideal melody, sublime in its steady flow towards an inevitable soaring climax. In more squarely measured phrases the Dutchman then asks Senta if she will pledge herself to him for ever, to which Senta responds with evident warmth, driving him to the exultant declaration that she is indeed the angel through whom his salvation might come. First, however, to the stormy motives associated with the power of the sea, he warns her of the dangers she will run by sharing his life. Her answer, delivered in the typical high-soaring phrases of Wagner's redeemer-heroines, is to promise everlasting loyalty. The music of this remarkably subtle and complex duet then gathers pace to culminate in a final outburst of ecstasy, '*Was ist's das mächtig in mir lebet*', which is unleashed in a manner that bears Wagner's hall-mark in every bar.

Having attained the highest possible pitch of excitement, the composer has no other recourse than to bring back Daland to reduce the emotional heat with his mundane question: have they agreed to marry? Their affirmative answer leads to a brief trio in which the deal is clinched, all agree to join the festivities outside, and the orchestra leads the way into the final scene. To achieve Wagner's original one-act scheme is a simple matter, the excision of a dozen bars from the Act II postlude which are repeated as the opening to the prelude of Act III. Several now familiar themes are combined here, notably the sailors' song which gradually becomes dominant. It is the sailors, in fact, who open the scene with a lusty rendering of the song, emphasising its strong rhythm as they dance clumsily on the deck of the Norwegian ship. They are soon joined by the girls from Daland's house, who make their contribution to a fairly conventional chorus by offering food and drink to their men. There are also some eerie orchestral contributions in response to the sailors' calls to the silent crew of the Dutch ship to join them. The girls, frightened by the stories the sailors tell them about the strange ship, decide to go home and return later, leaving the Norwegian crew to take up their song once more. This time the Dutch crew answer with their own sinister chorus, voicing the doubt that their gloomy captain will have any success in his search for a bride. Their song, appropriately accompanied by storm music, terrifies the Norwegian sailors, who hurry below deck after a vain attempt to outsing their rivals. Wagner's unique mastery of music associated with the sea enables him to give genuine distinction to this scene, which in other hands could easily have been mere routine choral padding.

The storm dies down as suddenly as it began, and the Dutchman motive sings out quietly on the horns over a string tremolando to be answered by the Redemption motive. The calm is quickly broken by agitated music in the strings heralding the arrival of Senta, followed by an almost hysterical Erik. Pleading with her to forget the Dutchman, Eric reminds her of the affection she once felt for him in an eloquent cavatina, '*Willst jenes Tags du nicht dich mehr entsinnen*'. Those over-

Above: Dancing girls decorate the production at the Staatstheater Kassel, 1976

zealous musical historians whom one might best describe as practising Wagnerites have dismissed this aria as superfluous, but the unprejudiced opera goer will welcome it as an example of the lyrical aspect of the composer's many-sided genius. The arrival of the Dutchman, who has overheard and misunderstood this exchange, leads into a brief trio based on a terse theme recently heard at the beginning of Erik's quarrel with Senta. Brevity is the soul of Wagner's genius when he decides to bring his works to an abrupt, shattering conclusion after what has sometimes seemed a leisurely journey.

In the course of the hectic finale, the entry of the Dutchman is marked *feroce* in the score, the trio simply *molto agitato*. The Dutchman declares he has lost his faith in God as well as woman's constancy, Senta protests her loyalty, and Erik sees the Devil's influence at work. In solemn phrases the Dutchman finally tells Senta of the dreadful fate from which she is spared, and it is proof of Wagner's dramatic mastery that he produces an overwhelming effect when he makes the Dutchman reveal his identity to Senta, even though the audience knows she has been aware of it all the time. All the musical strands of the work are drawn together in the final few minutes as the Dutchman boards his ship, which sets sail immediately, and Senta throws herself into the sea to redeem the man for whom her love is more than mortal. The music for the vision of Senta and the Dutchman rising heavenwards from the wrecked ship is the Redemption motive in its transfigured form as heard at the close of the overture, bringing poem and music full circle in the only conceivably right way to conclude a work which heralded the birth of music drama.

A Survey of Performances and Recordings

The première of *The Flying Dutchman* at the Dresden Court Theatre on January 2, 1843, was prepared in almost 'sweaty haste' to cash in on the success of *Rienzi*, making use of existing scenery from productions of other operas, and leaving Wagner little time to instruct the singers in his new dramatic philosophy. Depressed by the general incompetence of the company, he pinned his only hope of success on his leading lady, Wilhelmine Schröder-Devrient. He had first seen her on stage in Leipzig as Leonore in *Fidelio* in 1829, when he was at the impressionable age of sixteen and she, though only nine years his senior, was already famous thoughout Germany as the great singing actress who had done so much to popularise Beethoven's opera. 'After the performance', he recalled in his autobiography, 'I rushed to a friend's house and wrote her a short note in which I told her that from that moment my life had acquired its true significance, and that if in days to come she should ever hear my name praised in the world of Art, she must remember that she had that evening made me what I then swore it was my destiny to become.' It was also her singing in *I Capuleti e i Montecchi* which fired his early enthusiasm for Bellini.

When they met in Dresden in 1842, Wagner was delighted to find that Schröder-Devrient had not only kept this letter but could quote it word for word. Clearly they were equals in vanity, if in nothing else. The composer's account of his work with her on *The Flying Dutchman*, written down many years later, suggests that experience had soured his romantic enthusiasm, for he emphasised every artistic and personal fault he could find in his one-time idol. He assumed a tone of moral indignation when writing about her love affairs that ill became a man who had shamelessly seduced the wife of his close friend and benefactor. Even so, he was not able to deny that she had 'plunged into her study of her role as if it were a matter of life and death' and ultimately gave a magnificent performance as Senta.

Opposite: Harry Kupfer's production at Bayreuth in 1978 presents the Flying Dutchman (Simon Estes) as a figment of the sick imagination of Senta (Lisbeth Balsler), who dreams up his arrival on the ghost ship

The role of the Dutchman had to be entrusted to Johann Michael Wächter, a baritone whose 'distressing corpulence, broad fat face and extraordinary movements of arms and legs, which he managed to make look like mere stumps, drove my passionate Senta to despair'. Wagner's description, even if it is exaggerated, leaves no doubt that Wächter was fatally miscast. The bass Karl Risse sang Daland, and it would seem he was as dull a singer as Wächter, the tenor Reinhold the part of Erik. In addition to the deficiencies of the male side of the cast, the première suffered from the theatre's inability to stage the all-important scenic effects that Wagner demanded. 'The loudest raging of the orchestra', he complained, 'did not rouse the sea from its dead calm nor the phantom ship in its cautious rocking.' He was disappointed, therefore, when his opera was withdrawn after only four performances, though he was probably not so surprised as he pretended. His dramatic and theatrical senses must have already been telling him that his own new approach to music drama could only be fulfilled through a corresponding revitalising of the techniques of stage pre-sentation.

Although Dresden did not revive it until twenty-two years later, when it established itself as one of the most popular works in the repertoire, and although the Berlin production of 1844 also secured only four performances before it disappeared until 1869, *The Flying Dutchman* enjoyed considerable success elsewhere. It was first appreciated in Kassel on June 5, 1843, only five months after the Dresden failure, when the splendid conducting of Louis (Ludwig) Spohr helped to secure it a good run during the season there. It was no less warmly acclaimed about the same time in Riga, where the theatre management and the audience clearly demonstrated they bore no ill-feeling towards the man who had deserted them four years earlier to escape his creditors. Then there were the historic performances in Zürich during the winter of 1851–52, for which Wagner, who conducted, revised some of the orchestration and changed the ending of the overture to the form we know today.

The Flying Dutchman was the first Wagner opera to reach London, where it was given at Drury Lane on July 23, 1870, sung in Italian as *L'Olandese dannato* with Sir Charles Santley (Dutchman), Ilma di Murska (Senta), Allan James Foley (Daland), Julius Perotti (Erik) and Luigi Arditi conducting.

Above: Rudolf Bockelmann (centre) during a rehearsal for the 1933 Bayreuth production with Winifred Wagner and Karl Elmendorff

Herman Klein, who was to become a distinguished critic in both London and New York but was then a mere fourteen-year-old enthusiast, described the music as 'unlike anything I had ever heard. The overture, the storm music of the first act, the picture of the clumsy ship moving about the stage, and Senta's ballad were the things that dwelt most clearly in my memory.' Another report mentions that some members of the audience laughed during the scene in which Senta and the Dutchman stand motionless at their first meeting. The work arrived at the Royal Opera House, Covent Garden, on June 16, 1877, again in Italian but this time as *Il Vascello fantasma*, with Victor Maurel (Dutchman), Emma Albani (Senta), Anacleto Bagaggiolo (Daland) and Fernando Carpi (Erik) and Auguste Vianesi conducting.

In the United States *The Flying Dutchman* was also given in Italian, at the Philadelphia Academy of Music on November 8, 1876, with Eugenia Pappenheim as Senta. The following year, on January 26, Clara Louise Kellogg presented it in English at the New York Academy of Music, singing Senta herself with a cast of nonentities including a George Conly as Daland. This unfortunate bass eventually died by drowning, a fact which Miss Kellogg recorded in her autobiography without apparently realising its irony. The opera was finally presented in German at the Metropolitan Opera on November 27, 1889, with Theodor Reichmann (Dutchman), Sophie Wiesner (Senta), Emil Fischer (Daland), Paul Kalisch (Erik) and Anton Seidl conducting. Distinguished interpreters of the Dutchman also include Anton van Rooy, Friedrich Schorr, Rudolf Bockelmann, Herbert Janssen, Joel Berglund, Hans Hotter, Hermann Uhde, George London, David Ward and Norman Bailey, who first sang the role at Linz in 1962 and has subsequently enjoyed world-wide acclaim not only in Britain but from Vienna and Hamburg to Chicago and New York. Famous Sentas have included Emmy Destinn, Maria Müller, Frida Leider, Kirsten Flagstad, Astrid Varnay, Leonie Rysanek, Sylvia Fisher, Anja Silja and Gwyneth Jones.

Productions of the drama have varied radically over the years in accordance with advancing stage techniques and changing tastes. It is curious that Bayreuth did not present *The Flying Dutchman* until 1901, though at least amends were made for this neglect by playing it in the one-act form that Wagner had always intended. He was such a perfectionist, with very definite ideas about visual presentation, that he would no doubt have damned far more productions than he would have praised, and it is certain that he would never have completely approved of any performance he did not supervise himself. It is impossible even to imagine what he would have said of the 1978 Bayreuth production by Harry Kupfer, which reduced the Dutchman to a mere figment of Senta's imagination and ended with her throwing herself from an upstairs window into the street. The production rejected the whole concept of redemption, so it was found more convenient to revert to the first version of the score in which the Redemption motive does not feature in transfigured form at the close of the overture and the very end of the opera.

Left: Kirsten Flagstad, one of the most popular Sentas

On the other hand, Wagner would probably have been delighted that the long-playing gramophone record has made his works available to every home in performances musically superior to most that are heard in the opera house. His *Ring* cycle, even, can be swallowed whole by a listener with sufficient powers of concentration, and despite his lifelong concern with matters of staging there is much to be said for allowing the imagination to conjure up for itself the dramatic action and visual setting so vividly suggested by his music. The storm episodes of *The Flying Dutchman*, the whirling of the spinning wheels and the mystical relationship between Senta and the Dutchman are so explicit in the music that they are indeed often more real when experienced through sound alone than when producers attempt to realise them in the theatre.

Of the six rival versions, the oldest is generally considered the most successful as a whole. This was recorded live at Bayreuth in 1955, with Joseph Keilberth conducting the Festspielhaus

Above: Final moment in the 1969 Sadler's Wells production

forces with admirable dramatic urgency. The occasional imperfections inevitable in a recording of a stage performance are of only minimal importance, because a sense of mounting excitement is achieved which eludes even the most committed cast working in studio conditions, while the use of the one-act version maintains absolute continuity. Hermann Uhde is a fine Dutchman, singing with smooth command of legato and a salty sense of character encompassing the depth of grief and the height of exaltation when the hope of redemption seems to be finally at hand. His Senta, Astrid Varnay, sings with powerful conviction and spacious phrasing even when her voice sounds sometimes rough at the edges. Ludwig Weber, though a little past his prime, makes an impressive Daland, and the only disappointment is the Erik of Josef Traxel, who ignores Wagner's warning against sounding over-sentimental.

The richest sound is heard on the most recent recording, which brings Georg Solti conducting the Chicago Symphony Orchestra and Chorus with a cast headed by Norman Bailey, who offers an intelligently thought out portrayal of the Dutchman, and Janis Martin, who presents a strongly sung Senta which is unfortunately lacking in dramatic stature. Martti Talvela is the most healthy-voiced of Dalands, a little too noble perhaps for the bourgeois Norwegian skipper, and René Kollo sounds a virile Erik. The set featuring Otto Klemperer with the New Philharmonia Orchestra and the BBC Chorus opens in overwhelming style with a masterly account of the overture, and his cast includes Theo Adam, who has the right brooding presence for the Dutchman, and, as with the Solti version, Talvela as Daland. Unfortunately Anja Silja, despite her excitingly positive portrayal of Senta, lapses into moments of squally tone that would send any musically sensitive Dutchman straight back to sea hoping for better luck in another seven years' time.

A second recording of an actual Bayreuth performance, made in 1971, found the Festspielhaus chorus responding with poor discipline to the conducting of Karl Böhm, and neither Thomas Stewart as the Dutchman nor Gwyneth Jones as Senta was in good vocal condition at the time. Another disappointing set, in which Franz Konwitschny conducts the Deutsche Opera Orchestra and Chorus, has only the sensitive performance of Dietrich Fischer-Dieskau as the Dutchman to recommend it. A far worthier version is one which combines soloists from Metropolitan Opera revivals of the mid-sixties with the Orchestra and Chorus of the Royal Opera House, Covent Garden, conducted by Antal Dorati. Leonie Rysanek sings with notable accomplishment as Senta, Giorgio Tozzi gives an effective touch of bluff humour to his portrayal of Daland, and Karl Liebl is perhaps the most eloquent of all Eriks on record. Sadly, however, George London lacks any real distinction as the Dutchman.

There is a fairly wide choice, then, of *Flying Dutchman* recordings, though none is without its flaws. Reaction to singers is always a highly personal matter, so that all the artists mentioned here will find their champions, and there will be similar diversity of opinion regarding the six eminent conductors. Quality of recording is another important consideration. The Keilberth version has continued to win the strongest support because it provides the most satisfactory balance of these various aspects, and also by virtue of its exhilarating theatrical atmosphere, a major factor in the performance of this particular work.

Libretto

TIME: THE EIGHTEENTH CENTURY

PLACE: NORWAY

English translation by Charles Osborne

AKT I

MATROSEN

Hojohe! Hallojo!

DALAND

Kein Zweifel! Sieben Meilen fort
Trieb uns der Sturm vom sichren Port.
So nah' dem Ziel nach langer Fahrt,
War mir der Streich noch aufgespart!

STEUERMANN

Ho! Kapitän!

DALAND

Am Bord bei euch, wie steht's?

STEUERMANN

Gut, Kapitän! Wir haben sichren
Grund.

DALAND

Sandwike ist's! Genau kenn' ich die
Bucht.
Verwünscht! Schon sah am Ufer ich
mein Haus,
Senta, mein Kind, glaubt ich schon zu
umarmen:
Da bläst es aus dem Teufelsloch heraus!
Wer baut auf Wind, baut auf Satans
Erbarmen!
Was hilft's? Geduld! Der Sturm lässt
nach;
Wenn so er tobte, währt's nicht lang.
He, Bursche! Lange war't ihr wach;
Zur Ruhe denn! Mir ist nicht bang.

ACT I

(*A seashore, with steep cliffs. A violent storm is raging. Daland's ship has taken shelter in the bay, and Daland has gone ashore to reconnoitre. Sailors are busy furling sails, and throwing ropes to secure the ship to land.*)

SAILORS

Hoyohey!
Halloho!

DALAND

There's no doubt. The storm has driven us seven miles from the safety of our port. So close to home after a long journey, and then this stroke of bad luck.

HELMSMAN

Hey, Captain!

DALAND

How's everything on board?

HELMSMAN

Fine, Captain. We're safely landed.

DALAND

This is Sandwike. I know this bay well. Confound it! I could already see my house on shore, and I was expecting soon to embrace Senta, my child. But then this wind came blowing out of hell. Whoever trusts the wind trusts in the mercy of Satan! (*He goes aboard.*) It can't be helped. Patience, the storm will soon pass. When it's so fierce, it doesn't last long. Hey, lads, you've been keeping watch a long time. Have a rest now. I'm not worried.

(*The crew descends into the hold.*)

Nun, Steuermann, die Wache nimmst du
wohl für mich?
Gefahr ist nicht, doch gut ist's, wenn du
wachst.

STEUERMANN

Seid ausser Sorg! Schlaft ruhig,
Kapitän!

Mit Gewitter und Sturm aus fernem
Meer,
Mein Mädel, bin dir nah!
Über turmhohe Flut vom Süden her,
Mein Mädel, ich bin da!
Mein Mädel, wenn nicht Südwind wär',
Ich nimmer wohl käm' zu dir:
Ach, lieber Südwind, blas noch mehr!
Mein Mädel verlangt nach mir!
Ho ho jo! Hallohoho!
Von des Südens Gestad', aus weitem
Land
Ich hab' an dich gedacht!
Durch Gewitter und Meer vom
Mohrenstrand
Hab' dir 'was mitgebracht.
Mein Mädel, preis' den Südwind hoch,
Ich bring' dir ein gülden Band:
Ach, lieber Südwind, blase doch!
Mein Mädel hätt' gern den Tand.
Hoho! Je holla ho!

Mein Mädel, wenn nicht Südwind wär'.

HOLLÄNDER

Die Frist ist um,
Und abermals verstrichen sind sieben
Jahr'.
Voll Überdruss wirft mich das Meer
an's Land.

Now, helmsman, you'll keep watch for
me? There's no danger, but it's best you
keep alert.

HELMSMAN

Don't you worry. Have a good sleep,
Captain.

(*Daland goes into his cabin. The Helmsman
stays alone on deck.*)

Through storms, from distant seas, I
draw near to you, my maiden. Over
mountainous waves, from the south, my
maiden, I've arrived. My maiden, if
there were no south wind, I could never
come to you. Oh, dear south wind,
blow more strongly. My maiden longs
for me! Ho yo ho, Hallohoho.

On southern shores, in distant lands, I
thought of you. Through storm and
sea, from Moorish shores, I have
brought something for you. My maiden,
give praise to the south wind, for I
bring you a golden ring. Oh, dear south
wind, blow on, my maiden would like to
have her trinket. Hoho! Holloho!

(*He falls asleep. The storm increases in
intensity again, and the sky darkens. The
Flying Dutchman's ship rapidly approaches,
and drops anchor with a tremendous crash
close to the Norwegian ship. The Helmsman
stirs in his sleep, and murmurs:*)

My maiden, if there were no south wind
. . .

(*He goes back to sleep. The ghostly crew of
the Dutchman furl their sails, as the
Dutchman himself steps ashore.*)

DUTCHMAN

The term is up. Another seven years
have passed. Full of weariness, the
ocean throws me onto land. Ha, proud
ocean! In a short time you will carry me

Ha! Stolzer Ozean!
In kurzer Frist sollst du mich wieder
tragen!
Dein Trotz ist beugsam,
Doch ewig meine Qual.
Das Heil, das auf dem Land ich suche,
Nie werd' ich es finden!
Euch, des Weltmeers Fluten,
Bleib' ich getreu,
Bis eure letzte Welle sich bricht,
Und euer letztes Nass versiegt.
Wie oft in Meeres tiefsten Schlund
Stürzt' ich voll Sehnsucht mich hinab,
Doch ach! den Tod, ich fand ihn nicht!
Da, wo der Schiffe furchtbar' Grab,
Trieb mein Schiff ich zum
Klippengrund:
Doch ach! mein Grab, es schloss sich
nicht.
Verhöhnend droht' ich dem Piraten,
In wildem Kampfe hofft' ich Tod:
Hier, rief ich, zeige deine Taten,
Von Schätzen voll ist Schiff und Boot!
Doch ach! des Meers' barbar'scher Sohn
Schlägt bang das Kreuz und flieht
davon!
Wie oft in Meeres tiefsten Schlund
Stürzt' ich voll Sehnsucht mich hinab!
Da, wo der Schiffe furchtbar' Grab,
Trieb mein Schiff ich zum
Klippengrund:
Nirgends ein Grab! Niemals der Tod!
Dies der Verdammnis Schreckgebot.
Dich frage ich, gepriesner Engel Gottes,
Der meines Heils Bedingung mir
gewann:
War ich Unsel'ger Spielwerk deines
Spottes,
Als die Erlösung du mir zeigtest an?
Dich frage ich, *etc.*
Vergeb'ne Hoffnung! Furchtbar eitler
Wahn!
Um ew'ge Treu auf Erden ist's getan!

again. Your challenge is ever-changing,
but my torment is eternal. The grace
that I seek on land, I shall never find.
To you, tides of the ocean, I shall
remain true, until your last wave breaks
and your last drop of water dries. How
often into the sea's deepest depths have
I hurled myself in yearning, but, alas, I
could not find death. Onto the rocks
where many a ship has found its
fearsome grave, I drove my vessel. But,
alas, my grave would never close. With
taunts I challenged pirates, hoping for
death in fierce combat. 'Here', I cried,
'show me your courage. My ship is full
of treasure.' Alas, the sea's barbaric sons
anxiously crossed themselves and fled.
How often into the sea's deepest depths
have I hurled myself in yearning! Onto
the rocks where many a ship has found
its fearful grave, I drove my vessel.
Nowhere a grave! Never my death!
This is the dreadful decree of
damnation.

I ask you, most blessed angel of God,
who won for me the terms of my
salvation, was I the unhappy plaything
of your mockery when you showed me
the possibility of redemption?

Vain hope! Dreadful empty fancy! There
is no eternal fidelity to be found on
earth.

Nur eine Hoffnung soll mir bleiben,
Nur eine unerschüttert steh'n:
Solang' der Erde Keim' auch treiben,
So muss sie doch zu Grunde geh'n!
Tag des Gerichtes! Jüngster Tag!
Wann brichst du an in meine Nacht?
Wann dröhnt er, der Vernichtungs
Schlag,
Mit dem die Welt zusammen kracht?
Wann alle Toten aufersteh'n,
Dann werde ich in nichts vergeh'n.
Ihr Welten, endet euren Lauf!
Ew'ge Vernichtung, nimm mich auf!

Only one hope remains to me, only one
remains unshattered. Although earth's
seeds may continue to flourish, one day
it must all come to an end. Day of
judgment! Last day! When will you
come to end my night? When will the
knell of doom sound with which the
earth shall be destroyed? When all the
dead arise, then shall I become
nothingness. Planets, end your course!
Eternal oblivion, take me.

MANNSCHAFT DES HOLLÄNDERS

Ew'ge Vernichtung, nimm uns auf!

THE DUTCHMAN'S CREW

Eternal oblivion, take us.

(Daland comes out of his cabin, and sees the strange ship.)

DALAND

He! Holla! Steuermann!

DALAND

Hey, Helmsman!

STEUERMANN

'Sist nichts—'sist nichts—
"Ach, lieber Südwind, blas' noch mehr,
Mein Mädel—"

HELMSMAN

'S all right, s' all right. Ah, dear south
wind, blow on, my maiden . . .

DALAND

Du siehst nichts?
Gelt, du wachest brav, mein Bursch!
Dort liegt ein Schiff.
Wie lange schliefst du schon?

DALAND

You see nothing? Heavens, what a great
watch you are, my lad. A ship is lying
there. How long have you been
sleeping?

STEUERMANN

Zum Teufel auch! Verzeiht mir,
Kapitän!
Wer da? . . . Wer da?

HELMSMAN

The devil take me! I'm sorry, Captain.

(He calls to the other ship.)

Who's there?

(A long pause.)

DALAND

Es scheint, sie sind gerad' so faul, als
wir.

DALAND

It seems they're just as lazy as we are.

STEUERMANN

Gebt Antwort!
Schiff und Flagge?

DALAND

Lass ab! Mich dünkt, ich seh' den
Kapitän!
He! Holla! Seemann!
Nenne dich! wess Landes?

HOLLÄNDER

Weit komm' ich her;
Verwehrt bei Sturm und Wetter
Ihr mir den Ankerplatz?

DALAND

Behüt es Gott!
Gastfreundschaft kennt der Seemann!
Wer bist du?

HOLLÄNDER

Holländer.

DALAND

Gott zum Gruss!
So trieb auch dich der Sturm
Aus diesen nackten Felsenstrand?
Mir ging's nicht besser;
Wenig Meilen nur von hier ist meine
Heimat,
Fast erreicht, musst' ich auf's neu'
Mich von ihr wenden.
Sag', woher kommst du?
Hast Schaden du genommen?

HOLLÄNDER

Mein Schiff ist fest,
Es leidet keinen Schaden.
Durch Sturm und bösen Wind
verschlagen,
Irr' auf den Wassern ich umher.
Wie lange? weiss ich kaum zu sagen,
Schon zähl' ich nicht die Jahre mehr.

HELMSMAN

Answer me! What ship and flag?

DALAND

Hold on, I think I see the Captain.
Hey, there, seaman! What's your name?
What country?

DUTCHMAN

I've come a great distance. Would you
refuse me anchorage in this stormy
weather?

DALAND

God forbid! Seaman know how to be
hospitable.
Who are you?

DUTCHMAN.

Dutchman.

DALAND

Greetings to you. So the storm drove
you also to this barren, rocky beach. I
fared no better. But my home is only a
few miles from here; I was almost there
when I had to turn away from it. Tell
me, where have you come from? Have
you suffered damage?

DUTCHMAN

My ship is safe, she suffered no damage.
Driven on by storm and angry winds, I
roam across the waters. How long I can
hardly say, for I no longer count the
years. It would be impossible for me to
name all the countries I've found: the
only one for which I'm burning, I

Unmöglich dünkt mich's, dass ich nenne
Die Länder alle, die ich fand:
Das eine nur, nach dem ich brenne,
Ich find' es nicht, mein Heimatland!
Vergönne mir auf kurze Frist dein Haus
Und deine Freundschaft soll dich nicht gereu'n.
Mit Schätzen aller Gegenden und Zonen
Ist reich mein Schiff beladen:
Willst du handeln,
So sollst du sicher deines Vorteils sein.

DALAND

Wie wunderbar! Soll deinem Wort ich glauben?
Ein Unstern, scheint's, hat dich bis jetzt verfolgt.
Um dir zu frommen, biet' ich, was ich kann,
Doch darf ich fragen,
Was dein Schiff enthält?

HOLLÄNDER

Die seltensten der Schätze sollst du seh'n
Kostbare Perlen, edelstes Gestein.
Blick' hin, und überzeuge dich vom Werte des Preises,
Den ich für ein gastlich' Dach dir biete

DALAND

Wie? Ist's möglich? Diese Schätze!
Wer ist so reich, den Preis dafür zu bieten?

HOLLÄNDER

Den Preis? Soeben hab' ich ihn genannt
Dies für das Obdach einer einz'ger Nacht!
Doch was du siehst, ist nur der kleinste Teil
Von dem, was meines Schiffes Raum verschliesst.

cannot find—my homeland. Let me stay at your house for a short time, and you'll not regret your friendliness. With treasures from all lands and zones my ship is richly laden. If you will do this, you can be sure to profit by it.

DALAND

How strange! Can I believe your words? Ill-luck, it seems, has pursued you until now. I shall do what I can to help you, but may I ask what your ship contains?

DUTCHMAN

The rarest of treasures you shall see, priceless pearls, precious stones. Look, and convince yourself of their value. I offer them to you for a hospitable roof.

DALAND

(Gazes in amazement at the contents of a chest which, on a signal from the Dutchman, some of his crew have brought ashore.)

What? Is it possible? Such treasures! Who is so rich as to offer such a price?

DUTCHMAN

So much? It is just as I have said: all this in return for one night's shelter. Yet, what you see is only the smallest portion of what is stowed away on my ship. Of what use is treasure? I have neither wife nor child, and my homeland I can never find. All my

Was frommt der Schatz? Ich habe
weder Weib noch Kind,
und meine Heimat find' ich nie!
All' meinen Reichtum biet' ich dir,
Wenn bei den Deinen du mir neue
Heimat gibst.

DALAND

Was muss ich hören!

HOLLÄNDER

Hast du eine Tochter?

DALAND

Fürwahr, ein treues Kind.

HOLLÄNDER

Sie sei mein Weib!

DALAND

Wie? Hör' ich recht?
Meine Tochter sein Weib?
Er selbst spricht aus den Gedanken!
Fast fürcht' ich, wenn unentschlossen
ich bleib',
Er müsst' im Vorsatze wanken.
Wüsst' ich, ob ich wach' oder träume?
Kann ein Eidam willkommener sein?
Ein Tor, wenn das Glück ich
versäume!
Voll Entzücken schlage ich ein.

HOLLÄNDER

Ach, ohne Weib, ohne Kind bin ich,
nichts fesselt mich an die Erde.
Rastlos verfolgte das Schicksal mich, die
Qual nur war mir Gefährte.
Nie werd' ich die Heimat erreichen,
was frommt mir der Güter Gewinn?
Lässt du zu dem Bund dich erweichen,
O! so nimm meine Schätze dahin!

riches I offer you, if among your people
you will give me a new homeland.

DALAND

What do I hear?

DUTCHMAN

Do you have a daughter?

DALAND

Indeed, yes, a good child.

DUTCHMAN

Make her my wife!

DALAND

What? Do I hear rightly? Make my
daughter his wife? It was he who
uttered the thought. I almost fear that,
if I remain undecided, he may change
his mind. I'm not sure whether I'm
awake or dreaming. Could any son-in-
law be more welcome? I'd be a fool to
pass up this good luck. I'm delighted to
agree.

DUTCHMAN

Ah, I am without wife, without child,
and nothing binds me to this earth.
Relentlessly fate has pursued me, pain
alone was my companion. Never shall I
reach my homeland, of what avail to me
are riches. Consent to this marriage, and
you may take all my riches.

DALAND

Wohl, Fremdling, hab' ich eine schöne
Tochter,
Mit treuer Kindeslieb' ergeben mir:
Sie ist mein Stolz, das höchste meiner
Güter,
Mein Trost im Unglück, meine Freud'
im Glück.

HOLLÄNDER

Dem Vater stets bewahr' sie ihre Liebe!
Ihm treu, wird sie auch treu dem Gatten
sein.

DALAND

Du gibst Juwelen, unschätzbare Perlen,
Das höchste Kleinod doch, ein treues
Weib—

HOLLÄNDER

Du gibst es mir?

DALAND

Ich gebe dir mein Wort.
Mich rührt dein Los;
Freigebig, wie du bist,
Zeigst Edelmut und hohen Sinn du
mir:
Den Eidam wünscht' ich so,
Und wär' dein Gut auch nicht so reich,
Wählt ich doch keinen andren!

HOLLÄNDER

Hab' Dank!
Werd' ich die Tochter heut' noch seh'n?

DALAND

Der nächste günst'ge Wind
Bringt uns nach Haus;
Du sollst sie seh'n.
Und wenn sie dir gefällt—

DALAND

True, stranger, I have a beautiful
daughter, devoted to me with the true
love of a child. She is my pride, the
dearest of my possessions, my comfort
in sorrow and my joy in happiness.

DUTCHMAN

Her love for her father is already
proven. True to him, she will also be
true to her husband.

DALAND

You give jewels, priceless pearls, but
the most precious gem, a faithful wife—

DUTCHMAN

You will give to me?

DALAND

I give you my word. I am moved by
your loss. Generous as you are, and
showing such nobility of mind, just so
would I have my son-in-law be. Even if
you were not too rich, I would choose
no other.

DUTCHMAN

I thank you. Shall I see your daughter
today?

DALAND

The next fair wind will bring us home.
You shall see her, and if she pleases
you—

HOLLÄNDER

So ist sie mein.
Wird sie mein Engel sein?
Wenn aus der Qualen Schreckgewalten
Die Sehnsucht nach dem Heil mich
treibt,
Ist mir's erlaubt, mich festzuhalten
An einer Hoffnung, die mir bleibt!
Darf ich in jenem Wahn noch
schmachten,
Dass sich ein Engel mir erweicht?
Der qualen, die mein Haupt umnochten,
Ersehntes Zeil hätt ich erreicht?
Ach, ohne Hoffnung, wie ich bin,
Geb' ich der Hoffnung doch mich hin.

DALAND

Gepriesen seid, des
Sturms Gewalten,
Die ihr an diesen Strand mich triebt!
Fürwahr, bloss hab'ich fest zuhalten was
sich so schön von selbst mir gibt.
Die ihn an diese Küste brachten,
Ihr Winde, sollt gesegnet sein! Ja,
wonach alle Väter trachten,
ein reicher Eidam, er ist mein!
Ja, dem Mann mit Gut und hohen Sinn
Geb' froh ich Haus und Tochter hin!

STEUERMANN

Südwind! Südwind!
Ach, lieber Südwind, blas' noch mehr!

MATROSEN

Ho ho!

DALAND

Du siehst, das Glück ist günstig dir;
Der Wind ist gut, die See in Ruh'.
Sogleich die Anker lichten wir,
Und segeln froh der Heimat zu.

DUTCHMAN

She shall be mine.

(Aside.)

Will she be my angel?
When from the terrors of my anguish
My yearning for grace releases me, am I
allowed to cling to the one hope that
remains to me? May I indulge the vain
fancy that some angel will smile on me?
The anguish that clouds my mind, is it
really to end at last? Ah, without hope
as I am, I still give way to hope.

DALAND

Praised be the fierce storm which drove
me to this shore. Truly, I have only
now to grasp what has been so freely
offered to me. You winds who brought
him here, my blessing on you. Ha, what
every father desires, a wealthy son-in-
law, is mine. I give my house and my
daughter joyfully to a man of such
wealth and noble mind.

HELMSMAN

South wind! South wind! 'Ah, dear
south wind, blow on'.

SAILORS

Ho! Ho!

DALAND

You see, good fortune is with you. The
wind is fair, the sea is calm. We'll weigh
anchor immediately, and sail joyfully
home.

HOLLÄNDER

Darf ich dich bitten, so segelst du
voran;
Der Wind ist frisch, doch meine
Mannschaft müd';
Ich gönn' ihr kurze Ruh', und folge
dann!

DALAND

Doch, unser Wind?

HOLLÄNDER

Er bläst noch lang' aus Sud!
Mein Schiff ist schnell, es holt dich
sicher ein.

DALAND

Du glaubst? Wohlan, es möge denn so
sein!
Leb' wohl! Mögst heute du mein Kind
noch seh'n!

HOLLÄNDER

Gewiss!

DALAND

Hei! Wie die Segel schon sich bläh'n!
Hallo! Hallo!
Frisch, Jungen, greifet an!

MATROSEN

Mit Gewitter und Sturm aus fernem
Meer,
Mein Mädel, bin dir nah!
Hurra! Über turmhohe Flut vom Süden
her,
Mein Mädel, ich bin da!
Hurra! Mein Mädel, wenn nicht
Sudwind wär',
Ich nimmer wohl käm zu dir:
Ach, lieber Südwind, blas' noch mehr!
Mein Mädel verlangt nach mir!

DUTCHMAN

May I ask you to sail on ahead? The
wind is fresh, but my crew is tired. I'll
give them a little rest, then follow you.

DALAND

But our wind?

DUTCHMAN

It will blow for a long time from the
south. My ship is fast, so we'll overtake
you.

DALAND

You think so? Very well, let it be as
you say. Farewell, you may still see my
child today.

DUTCHMAN

For certain.

DALAND

(Goes back on board.)

Ha, how the sail already billows. Hello,
hello, lads, look lively there.

SAILORS

Through storms, from distant seas, I
draw near to you, my maiden. Over
mountainous waves, from the south, my
maiden, I've arrived. My maiden, if
there were no south wind, I could never
come to you. Oh, dear south wind,
blow more strongly. My maiden longs
for me.

AKT II

ACT II

CHOR DER MÄDCHEN

Summ' und brumm', du gutes Rädchen,
Munter, munter dreh' dich um!
Spinne, spinne tausend Fädchen,
Gutes Rädchen, summ' und brumm'!
Mein Schatz ist auf dem Meere draus',
Er denkt nach Haus an's fromme Kind;
Mein gutes Rädchen, braus' und saus'!
Ach, gäbst du Wind, er käm'
geschwind!
Spinnt! Spinnt! Spinnt! Fleissig,
Mädchen!
Brumm'! Summ'! Gutes Rädchen!
Tra la ra.

MARY

Ei, fleissig! fleissig, wie sie spinnen!
Will jede sich den Schatz gewinnen.

MÄDCHEN

Frau Mary, still! Denn wohl ihr wisst,
Das Lied noch nicht zu Ende ist!

MARY

So singt! Dem Rädchen lässt's nicht
Ruh'.
Du aber, Senta, schweigst dazu?

MÄDCHEN

Summ und brumm', du gutes Rädchen,
Munter, munter, dreh' dich um!
Spinne, spinne tausend Fädchen,
Gutes Rädchen, summ' und brumm'!
Mein Schatz da draussen auf dem Meer,
Im Süden er viel Gold gewinnt;
Ach, gutes Rädchen, saus' noch mehr!
Er gibt's dem Kind, wenn's fleissig
spinnt!
Fleissig, Mädchen!

ACT II

(A room in Daland's house. On one wall is a portrait of a pale man with a dark beard, in black Spanish costume. Mary and a number of girls sit spinning. Apart from them, Senta sits, contemplating the portrait.)

CHORUS OF GIRLS

Hum and rumble, good wheel, merrily, merrily spin round. Spin, spin a thousand threads, good wheel hum and rumble. My love is out there on the sea, thinking of home and his beloved child. My good wheel, hum and buzz. Ah, if you could summon up wind, he'd quickly be here. Spin, spin industriously, girls. Tra la ra.

MARY

How busily they spin. Each of them wants to win a lover.

GIRLS

Be quiet, Mistress Mary, for you know well our song is not yet finished.

MARY

Then sing. It keeps the wheel from stopping. But Senta, you remain silent?

GIRLS

Hum and rumble, good wheel, merrily, merrily spin round. Spin, spin a thousand threads, good wheel, hum and rumble. My love out there on the sea has won a great deal of gold in the south. Oh, good wheel, buzz on. He'll give it to his beloved if I spin busily. Industriously, girls.

MARY

Du böses Kind! Wenn du nicht spinnst,
Vom Schatz du kein Geschenk
gewinnst.

MÄDCHEN

Sie hat's nicht not, dass sie sich eilt;
Ihr Schatz nicht auf dem Meere weilt.
Bringt er nicht Gold, bringt er doch
Wild,
Man weiss ja, was ein Jäger gilt!

MARY

Da seht ihr! Immer vor dem Bild!
Willst du dein ganzes junges Leben
Verträumen vor dem Konterfei?

SENTA

Was hast du Kunde mir gegeben,
Was mir erzählet, wer er sei? . . .
Der arme Mann!

MARY

Gott sei mit dir!

MÄDCHEN

Ei, ei! Ei, ei! Was hören wir!
Sie seufzet um den bleichen Mann!

MARY

Den Kopf verliert sie noch darum!

MÄDCHEN

Da sieht man, was ein Bild doch kann!

MARY

Nichts hilft es, wenn ich täglich
brumm'!
Komm! Senta! Wend' dich doch
herum!

MARY

(To Senta:)

You wicked child, if you don't spin you
won't get a present from your beloved.

GIRLS

She has no need to hurry. Her beloved
is not roaming across the seas. He
doesn't bring gold, only game. We
know that's all a hunter can afford.

(Senta hums a few bars of song to herself.)

MARY

You see her! Always in front of that
portrait. Will you spend the whole of
your young life dreaming in front of
that picture?

SENTA

Why did you tell me his story? Why did
you tell me who he was? The poor
man!

MARY

God protect you.

GIRLS

Eh, eh, what's this we hear? She's
sighing for that pale man.

MARY

She's lost her head over it.

GIRLS

You see what a picture can do!

MARY

Chiding her daily doesn't help.
Come, Senta! Turn 'round this way!

MÄDCHEN

Sie hört euch nicht! Sie ist verliebt!
Ei Ei! Wenn's nur nicht Händel gibt!
Denn Erik hat gar heisses Blut,
Dass er nur keinen Schaden tut!
Sagt nichts! Er schiesst sonst
wutentbrannt
Den Nebenbuhler von der Wand!

SENTA

O schweigt mit eurem tollen Lachen!
Wollt ihr mich ernstlich böse machen?

MÄDCHEN

Summ' und brumm', du gutes Rädchen,
Munter, munter dreh' dich um!
Spinne, spinne tausend Fädchen!
Gutes Rädchen, summ' und brumm'!

SENTA

O, macht dem dummen Lied ein Ende!
Es brummt und summt mir vor dem
Ohr.
Wollt ihr, dass ich mich zu euch wende,
So sucht was besseres hervor!

MÄDCHEN

Gut! Singe du!

SENTA

Hört, was ich rate:
Frau Mary singt uns die Ballade.

MARY

Bewahre Gott, das fehlte mir!
Den fliegenden Holländer lasst in Ruh'!

SENTA

Wie oft doch hört' ich sie von dir!
Ich sing' sie selbst! Hört, Mädchen, zu!
Lasst mich's euch recht zum Herzen
führen,
Des Ärmsten Los es muss euch rühren!

GIRLS

She doesn't hear you. She's in love. Eh,
eh, I hope there'll be no unpleasantness,
for Erik is hot-blooded. I hope there'll
be no harm done. Say nothing, or,
burning with fury, he'll knock his rival
off the wall.

SENTA

Be quiet. Do you want to make me
really angry with your foolish laughter?

GIRLS

Hum and rumble, good wheel, merrily,
merrily spin round. Spin, spin a
thousand threads, good wheel, hum and
rumble.

SENTA

Oh, make an end of your stupid song.
It's humming and buzzing in my ear. If
you want me to join you, find a better
one.

GIRLS

Fine! You sing!

SENTA

Listen to my suggestion: Mistress Mary
will sing us the Ballad.

MARY

God forbid, that's the last straw! Leave
the flying Dutchman in peace.

SENTA

But how often I have heard it from you.
I'll sing it myself. Listen, girls. Let me
really bring it to your hearts. The poor
man's fate will surely move you.

MÄDCHEN

Uns ist es recht!

SENTA

Merkt auf die Wort'!

MÄDCHEN

Dem Spinnrad Ruh'!

MARY

Ich spinne fort!

SENTA

Jo ho hoe! Jo ho ho hoe!
Traft ihr das Schiff im Meere an,
Blutrot die Segel, schwarz der Mast?
Auf hohem Bord der bleiche Mann,
Des Schiffes Herr, wacht ohne Rast.
Hui, wie saust der Wind!
Jo ho he!
Hui! Wie pfeift's im Tau!
Jo ho he!
Hui! Wie ein Pfeil fliegt er hin,
Ohne Ziel, ohne Rast, ohne Ruh!
Doch kann dem bleichen Manne
Erlösung einstens noch werden,
Fänd' er ein Weib, das bis in den Tod
Getreu ihm auf Erden.
Ach! wann wirst du,
Bleicher Seemann, sie finden?
Betet zum Himmel, dass bald
Ein Weib Treue ihm halt'!
Bei bösem Wind und Sturmeswut
Umsegeln wollt' er einst ein Kap;
Er flucht' und schwur mit tollem Mut:
In Ewigkeit lass' ich nicht ab!
Hui! Und Satan hört's!
Jo ho he!
Hui! nahm ihn bei'm Wort.
Jo ho he!
Hui! Und verdammt zieht er nun
Durch das Meer ohne Rast, ohne
Ruh'!

GIRLS

That's fine with us.

SENTA

Pay attention to the words.

GIRLS

Stop the spinning wheels.

MARY

I'll keep on spinning.

SENTA

Yohohoe, Yohohohoe!
Have you met upon the sea the ship
with blood-red sails and black mast?
High up on deck, the pallid man,
master of the ship, keeps watch without
rest.
Hui! How the wind shrieks!
Yohohe!
Hui! How it whistles in the rigging!
Yohohe!
Hui! He flies on like an arrow,
without a goal, without rest, without
peace.
Yet this pale man may one day find
salvation,
If he can find a wife, who would remain
true to him on this earth, until death!
Ah, when will you find her, pale seaman?
Pray to heaven that soon
he will find a faithful wife.
In angry winds and raging storms,
he once tried to sail around a cape.
Crazed with determination, he cursed
and swore:
'I'll keep on trying for eternity'.
Hui! And Satan heard him. Yohohe!
Hui! And took him at his word.
Yohohe!
Hui! And, accursed, he must sail
Across the seas without rest, without
peace!

Doch, dass der arme Mann
Noch Erlösung fände auf Erden,
Zeigt' Gottes Engel an,
Wie sein Heil ihm einst könne werden.
Ach! Könntest du,
Bleicher Seemann, es finden!
Betet zum Himmel, dass bald
Ein Weib Treue ihm halt'!

Vor Anker alle sieben Jahr',
Ein Weib zu frei'n, geht er an's Land;
Er freite alle sieben Jahr',
Noch nie ein treues Weib er fand.
Hui! "Die Segel auf!"
Jo ho he! Jo ho he!
Hui! "Den Anker los!"
Jo ho he! Jo ho he!
Hui! "Falsche Lieb', falsche Treu'!
Auf, in See, ohne Rast, ohne Ruh"!

MÄDCHEN

Ach! wo weilt sie,
Die dir Gottes Engel einst könnte
zeigen?
Wo triffst du sie, die bis in den Tod
Dir könne zeigen?

SENTA

Ich sei's, die dich durch ihre Treu'
erlöse!
Mög' Gottes Engel mich dir zeigen!
Durch mich sollst du das Heil
erreichen!

MARY UND MÄDCHEN

Hilf, Himmel! Senta! Senta!

ERIK

Senta! Willst du mich verderben?

MÄDCHEN

Helft, Erik, uns! Sie ist von Sinnen!

Yet, so that the poor man might at last
find redemption on earth,
An angel of God showed him how he
might attain his salvation:
Ah, if only, pale seaman, you could find
it.
Pray to heaven that soon
he will find a faithful wife.

At anchor every seven years,
He goes ashore to seek a wife.
He searches every seventh year,
but has never found a faithful wife.
Hui! 'Hoist the sails!' Yohohe!
Hui! 'Weigh anchor!' Yohohe!
Hui! 'False love, false faith,
Away, to sea, without rest, without
peace!'

GIRLS

Ah, where is she, who God's angel may
one day reveal?
Where will you meet her who will
remain true until death?

SENTA

It is I who will redeem you with my
fidelity!
May God's angel reveal me to you!
Through me you shall attain
redemption!

MARY AND GIRLS

Heaven help us! Senta! Senta!

ERIK

(As he enters.)

Senta! Do you want to destroy me?

GIRLS

Help, Erik, she's lost her senses.

MARY

Ich fühl' in mir das Blut gerinnen!
Abscheulich' Bild, du sollst hinaus!
Kommt nur der Vater erst nach Haus!

ERIK

Der Vater kommt.

SENTA

Der Vater kommt?

ERIK

Vom Felsen sah sein Schiff ich nah'n.

MARY

Nun seht, zu was eu'r Treiben frommt!
Im Hause is noch nichts getan!

MÄDCHEN

Sie sind daheim! Auf, eilt hinaus!

MARY

Halt! Halt! Ihr bleibet fein im Haus!
Das Schiffsvolk kommt mit leerem
Magen.
In Küch und Keller säumet nicht!

MÄDCHEN

Ach! Wieviel hab' ich ihn zu fragen!
Ich halte mich vor Neugier nicht!

MARY

Lasst euch nur von der Neugier plagen!
Vor allem geht an eure Pflicht!

MÄDCHEN

Schon gut! Sobald nur aufgetragen
Mich halt hier länge keine Pflicht!

MARY

I feel my blood run cold.
Loathsome portrait, you'll be thrown
out as soon as her father comes home.

ERIK

Her father's coming.

SENTA

My father's coming?

ERIK

From the cliffs I saw his ship
approaching.

MARY

Now see what your carrying on has led
to!
Nothing has been done yet in the house.

GIRLS

They've come home. Let's hurry out.

MARY

Stop! Stop! You must stay here.
The sailors will arrive with empty
stomachs.
Get busy in the kitchen and the cellar.

GIRLS

Oh, I have so much to ask him.
I can't contain my curiosity.

MARY

Just forget your curiosity,
your duty is more important than
anything else.

GIRLS

All right. As soon as they've been fed,
We'll have no further duty here.

ERIK

Bleib', Senta! Bleib' nur einen
Augenblick!
Aus meinen Qualen reisse mich!
Doch willst du, ach! so verdirb mich
ganz!

SENTA

Was ist . . . ? Was soll . . . ?

ERIK

O Senta, sprich, was aus mir werden
soll?
Dein Vater kommt: eh' wieder er
verreist,
Wird er vollbringen, was schon oft er
wollte.

SENTA

Und was meinst du?

ERIK

Dir einen Gatten geben!
Mein Herz, voll Treue bis zum Sterben,
Mein dürftig' Gut, mein Jägerglück:
Darf so um deine Hand ich werben?
Stösst mich dein Vater nicht zurück?
Wenn dann mein Herz im Jammer bricht,
Sag', Senta, wer dann für mich spricht?

SENTA

Ach, schweige, Erik, jetzt!
Lass mich hinaus, den Vater zu
begrüssen!
Wenn nicht, wie sonst, an Bord die
Tochter kommt,
Wird er nicht zürnen müssen?

ERIK

Du willst mich flieh'n?

ERIK

Stay, Senta, stay just for a moment.
Rescue me from my torment. Or would
you
rather destroy me completely?

SENTA

What is—what should—?

ERIK

Oh Senta, speak. What's to become of
me?
Your father's coming. But before he
departs again,
he will accomplish what he has often
intended . . .

SENTA

What do you mean?

ERIK

To give you a husband!
My heart, faithful until death,
my humble possessions, my hunter's
luck,
with these, may I ask for your hand?
Will not your father refuse me?
If then my heart breaks in anguish,
say, Senta, who then will speak for me?

SENTA

Ah, be silent now, Erik, Let me go
to greet my father.
If his daughter does not go on board as
usual,
will he not be angry?

ERIK

You want to run away from me?

SENTA

Ich muss zum Port!

ERIK

Du weichst mir aus?

SENTA

Ach, lass mich fort!

ERIK

Fliehst du zurück vor dieser Wunde,
Die du mir schlugst, dem Liebeswahn?
O, höre mich zu dieser Stunde!
Hör' meine letzte Frage an:
Wenn dieses Herz im Jammer bricht,
Wird's Senta sein, die für mich spricht?

SENTA

Wie? Zweifelst du an meinem Herzen?
Du zweifelst, ob ich gut dir bin?
O sag, was weckt dir solche Schmerzen?
Was trübt mit Argwohn deinen Sinn?

ERIK

Dein Vater ach! nach Schätzen geizt er nur!
Und Senta, du, wie dürft' auf dich ich
zählen?
Erfülltest du nur eine meiner Bitten?
Kränkst du mein Herz nicht jeden Tag?

SENTA

Dein Herz?

ERIK

Was soll ich denken? Jenes Bild?

SENTA

Das Bild?

ERIK

Lässt du von deiner Schwärmerei wohl
ab?

SENTA

I must go down to the port.

ERIK

You are avoiding me?

SENTA

Ah, let me go.

ERIK

You recoil from this wound
that you have inflicted, the madness of
love?
Oh, listen to me at this hour,
hear my last question:
When this heart breaks in anguish,
will it be Senta who speaks for me?

SENTA

What? Do you doubt my heart?
Do you doubt my fondness for you?
Oh say, what causes you such sorrow?
What stirs this suspicion in your heart?

ERIK

Your father, ah, he's only keen on
wealth,
And you, Senta, how can I count on you?
Have you granted even one of my pleas?
Do you not wound my heart every day?

SENTA

Your heart?

ERIK

What am I to think? That portrait—

SENTA

The portrait?

ERIK

Will you give up this day-dreaming?

SENTA

Kann meinem Blick
Teilnahme ich verwehren?

ERIK

Und die Ballade, heut' noch sangst du
sie!

SENTA

Ich bin ein Kind und weiss nicht, was
ich singe.
O sag, wie? fürchtest du ein Lied, ein
Bild?

ERIK

Du bist so bleich,
Sag', sollte ich's nicht fürchten?

SENTA

Soll mich des Ärmsten Schreckenslos
nicht rühren?

ERIK

Mein Leiden, Senta, rührt es dich nicht
mehr?

SENTA

O, prahle nicht! Was kann dein Leiden
sein?
Kennst jenes Unglücksel'gen Schicksal
du?
Fühlst du den Schmerz, den tiefen
Gram,
Mit dem herab auf mich er sieht?
Ach! was die Ruhe für ewig ihm nahm,
Wie schneidend' Weh durch's Herz mir
zieht!

ERIK

Weh' mir! Es mahnt mich mein
unsel'ger Traum!
Gott schütze dich! Satan hat dich
umgarnt!

SENTA

Can I withold sympathy from my
glance?

ERIK

And the ballad, you sang it again today!

SENTA

I am a child, and don't know what I'm
singing . . .
But tell me, why do you fear a song, a
portrait?

ERIK

You are so pale . . . tell me why I
should not fear it.

SENTA

Should I not be moved by that poor
man's fate?

ERIK

Don't my sorrows, Senta, move you
more?

SENTA

Oh, don't brag. What can your sorrows
be?
Do you know the fate of that unhappy
man?
Do you feel the pain, the deep sorrow
with which he looks down at me?
Ah! That which has robbed him of his
peace for ever
stabs an aching pain into my heart.

ERIK

Alas, that reminds me of my unhappy
dream.
God protect you, for Satan has ensnared
you.

SENTA

Was erschreckt dich so?

ERIK

Senta, lass dir vertrau'n!
Ein Traum ist's—hör' ihn zur Warnung
an!
Auf hohem Felsen lag' ich träumend,
Sah unter mir des Meeres Flut;
Die Brandung hört' ich, wie sie
schäumend
Am Ufer brach der Wogen Wut!
Ein fremdes Schiff am nahen Strande
Erblickt' ich, seltsam, wunderbar:
Zwei Männer nahten sich dem Lande,
Der ein', ich sah's, dein Vater war.

SENTA

Der andre?

ERIK

Wohl erkannt' ich ihn; mit schwarzem
Wams,
Die bleiche Mien' . . .

SENTA

Der düst're Blick . . .

ERIK

Der Seemann, er.

SENTA

Und ich?

ERIK

Du kamst vom Hause her,
Du flogst, den Vater zu begrüssen,
Doch kaum noch sah ich an dich
langen,
Du stürztest zu des Fremden Füssen.
Ich sah dich seine Knie umfangen—

SENTA

What frightens you so?

ERIK

Senta, let me tell you.
It was a dream. Take it as a warning.
On a high cliff, I lay dreaming,
watching the ocean's flood below me.
I heard the waves surging and foaming
as they broke in fury upon the shore.
Close to the shore, a strange ship
I spied, mysterious and weird.
Two men came ashore from it,
and one of them, I saw, was your father.

SENTA

The other?

ERIK

I knew him well,
his black doublet, his pallid features . . .

SENTA

And gloomy stare . . .

ERIK

(Pointing to the portrait.)

He was that seaman.

SENTA

And I—

ERIK

You came out from the house,
and ran to greet your father.
But I saw that, no sooner had you
reached him
when you fell at the stranger's feet,
and I saw you clasp his knees.

SENTA

Er hub mich auf . . .

ERIK

. . . an seine Brust.
Voll Inbrunst hingst du dich an ihn,
Du küsstest ihn mit heisser Lust.

SENTA

Und dann?

ERIK

Sah ich auf's Meer euch flieh'n.

SENTA

Er sucht mich auf! Ich muss ihn seh'n!
Mit ihm muss ich zu Grunde geh'n!

ERIK

Entsetzlich! Mir wird es klar!
Sie ist dahin! Mein Traum sprach wahr!

SENTA

Ach, möchtest du, bleicher Seemann, sie
finden!
Betet zum Himmel, dass bald ein Weib
Treue ihm—
Ha!

DALAND

Mein Kind, du siehst mich auf der
Schwelle:
Wie? Kein Umarmen, keinen Kuss?
Du bleibst gebannt an deiner Stelle?
Verdien' ich, Senta, solchen Gruss?

SENTA

(With rising excitement.)
He lifted me up . . .

ERIK

Into his arms.
Passionately you clung to him,
And kissed him with fervent desire.

SENTA

And then?

ERIK

I saw you both sail away.

SENTA

(In the greatest excitement.)
He seeks me out! I must see him!
With him I must perish.

ERIK

Oh, horror! Now all is clear to me.
She is lost. My dream was true.

(He rushes out in horror.)

SENTA

Ah, may you find her, pale seaman?
Pray to heaven that soon
a faithful wife he . . . Ha!

*(The Dutchman and Daland appear at the
door. The Dutchman and Senta gaze at each
other.)*

DALAND

My child, you see me here on the
threshold.
Well? No embrace? No kiss?
You stay rooted to the spot?
Do I deserve, Senta, such a greeting?

SENTA

Gott dir zum Gruss!
Mein Vater, sprich, wer ist der Fremde?

DALAND

Drängst du mich?
Mögst du, mein Kind, den fremden
Mann willkommen heissen!
Seemann ist er, gleich mir, das Gastrecht
spricht er an.
Lang' ohne Heimat, stets auf fernen,
weiten Reisen,
In fremden Landen er der Schätze viel
gewann.
Aus seinem Vaterland verwiesen,
Für einen Herd er reichlich lohnt.
Sprich, Senta, wird es dich verdriessen,
Wenn dieser Fremde bei uns wohnt'?

Sagt, hab' ich sie zuviel gepriesen?
Ihr seht sie selbst, ist sie Euch recht?
Soll ich von Lob noch überfliessen?
Gesteht, sie zieret ihr Geschlecht!

Mögst du, mein Kind, dem Manne
Freundlich dich erweisen,
Von deinem Herzen auch spricht
Holde Gab' er an:
Reich' ihm die Hand, denn Bräutigam
Sollst du ihn heissen!
Stimmst du dem Vater bei,
Ist morgen er dein Mann.
Sieh' dieses Band, sieh' diese Spangen!
Was er besitzt, macht dies gering.
Muss, teures Kind, dich's nicht
verlangen?
Dein ist es, wechselst du den Ring!
Doch keines spricht! Sollt' ich hier
lästig sein?
So ist's—am besten lass' ich sie allein.

SENTA

God's greeting, father. But tell me,
who is this stranger?

DALAND

Do you press me to tell you?
Will you, my child, offer this stranger a
warm welcome?
He is a seaman like myself, and he asks
for shelter.
Long without a homeland, always
travelling in distant parts,
in foreign lands he has won much
treasure.
Banished from his own country,
he will pay handsomely for a hearth.
Tell me, Senta, would you object
if this stranger were to live with us?

(To the Dutchman:)

Tell me, did I praise her too highly?
You see her yourself, does she please
you?
Need I continue to praise her?
Admit that she's a credit to her sex.

(To Senta:)

Will you, my child, be friendly to this
man?
From your heart he asks a holy gift.
Give him your hand, for Bridegroom
you should call him.
If you agree with your father,
tomorrow he will be your husband.
See this bracelet, see these buckles,
these are but the smallest part of his
possessions.
Surely, dear child, you would love to
have them?
They are yours, when you exchange
rings.
But no one speaks. Am I an intruder
here?
Well then, it's best I leave them alone.

(To Senta:)

131

Mögst du den edlen Mann gewinnen!
Glaub' mir, solch' Glück wird nimmer
neu.
Bleibt hier allein! Ich geh' von hinnen:
Glaub' mir, wie schön, so ist sie treu!

HOLLÄNDER

Wie aus der Ferne längst vergang'ner
Zeiten,
Spricht dieses Mädchens Bild zu mir:
Wie ich's geträumt seit bangen
Ewigkeiten,
Vor meinen Augen seh' ich's hier.
Wohl hub auch ich voll Sehnsucht
meine Blicke
Aus tiefer Nacht empor zu einem Weib:
Ein schlagend' Herz liess ach! mir
Satans Tücke,
Dass eingedenk ich meiner Qualen
bleib'.
Die düstre Glut, die hier ich fühle
brennen,
Sollt' ich Unseliger sie Liebe nennen?
Ach nein! Die Sehnsucht ist es nach dem
Heil,
Würd' es durch solchen Engel mir zu
teil!

SENTA

Versank ich jetzt in wunderbares Träumen?
Was ich erblicke, ist's ein Wahn?
Weilt' ich bisher in trügerischen
Räumen?
Brach des Erwachens Tag heut' an?
Er steht vor mir, mit leidenvollen
Zügen, es spricht sein unerhörter Gram
zu mir.
Kann tiefen Mitleids Stimme mich belügen?
Wie ich ihn oft geseh'n, so steht er hier.
Die Schmerzen, die in meinen Busen
brennen, Ach!
dies Verlangen, wie soll ich es nennen?
Wonach mit Sehnsucht es dich treibt,
das Heil, . . . würd' es, du Ärmster, dir
durch mich zu Teil!

May you win this noble man.
Believe me, such fortune will not come
again.

(To the Dutchman:)

Stay here with her. I'm going.
Believe me, she is as true as she is
beautiful.

(He leaves, slowly.)

DUTCHMAN

As from the depths of long forgotten
times,
this girl's image speaks to me.
What I have dreamed of, through
anxious, endless years,
I now see before my eyes.
Often I have raised my eyes in yearning
for a wife, throughout the deepest night.
But Satan's trickery left me only a
pounding heart
constantly to remind me of my misery.
The dull glow that here I feel burning,
Shall I, unhappy man, call it love?
Ah, no. It is the yearning for salvation.
May it be mine through such an angel.

SENTA

Am I deep in some wonderful dream?
What I see, is it an illusion?
Or have I been deluded until now,
and is this my day of awakening?
He stands before me, his look so full of
sorrow,
it speaks to me of inexpressible grief.
Can the voice of deep compassion be
deceiving me?
Just as I have often seen him, so he
stands here.
The sorrows that burn within my breast,
ah, this longing, how shall I name it?
That for which you yearn, salvation,
would you could achieve it, poor man,
through me.

HOLLÄNDER

Wirst du des Vaters Wahl nicht
schelten?
Was er versprach, wie, dürft' es gelten?
Du könntest dich für ewig mir ergeben,
und deine Hand dem Fremdling
reichtest du?
Soll finden ich, nach qualenvollem
Leben,
In deiner Treu' die lang ersehnte Ruh'?

SENTA

Wer du auch seist und welches das
Verderben,
Dem grausam dich dein Schicksal
konnte weih'n,
Was auch das Los, das ich mir sollt'
erwerben,
Gehorsam stets werd' ich dem Vater
sein!

HOLLÄNDER

So unbedingt, wie? Könnte dich
durchdringen
Für meine Leiden tiefstes Mitgefühl?

SENTA

O, welche Leiden! Könnt' ich Trost dir
bringen!

HOLLÄNDER

Welch' holder Klang im nächtigen
Gewühl!
Du bist ein Engel, eines Engels Liebe
Verworf'ne selbst zu trösten weiss!
Ach, wenn Erlösung mir zu hoffen
bliebe,
Allewiger, durch diese sei's!

SENTA

Ach, wenn Erlösung ihm zu hoffen
bliebe,
Allewiger, durch mich nur sei's!

DUTCHMAN

Do you have no objection to your
father's choice?
What he promised, may it be so?
Could you give yourself to me for ever,
Give your hand to me, a stranger?
Shall I, after a life full of torment, find
in your faithfulness, my long sought
rest?

SENTA

Whoever you are, and whatever the fate
To which cruel destiny has condemned
you,
And whatever I may bring upon myself,
I shall always be obedient to my father.

DUTCHMAN

So positive? Are you really moved
by my suffering, to such deep
sympathy?

SENTA

(Aside:)

Oh, what sorrow. If only I could
comfort you.

DUTCHMAN

(Overhearing her:)

What a wonderful sound to ease my
night of pain.
You are an angel. An angel's love
can comfort even the rejected.
Ah, if hope of salvation still remains to
me,
Eternal God, let it come through her.

SENTA

(Aside:)

Ah, if hope of salvation still remains to
him,
Eternal God, let it come through me.

133

HOLLÄNDER

Ach! könntest das Geschick du ahnen,
Dem dann mit mir du angehörst,
Dich würd' es an das Opfer mahnen,
Das du mir bringst, wenn Treu' du
schwörst!
Es flöhe schaudernd deine Jugend
Dem Lose, dem du sie willst weih'n,
Nennst du des Weibes schönste
Tugend,
Nennst ew'ge Treue du nicht dein!

SENTA

Wohl kenn' ich Weibes heil'ge Pflichten;
Sei drum getrost, unsel'ger Mann!
Lass über die das Schicksal richten,
Die seinem Spruche trotzen kann!
In meines Herzens höchster Reine
Kenn' ich der Treue Hochgebot.
Wem ich sie weih', schenk' ich die eine:
Die Treue bis zum Tod!

HOLLÄNDER

Ein heil'ger Balsam meinen Wunden
dem Schwur, dem hohen Wort
entfliesst.
Hört es,
mein Heil hab'ich gefunden,
Mächte,
die ihr zurück mich stiesst!
Du Stern des Unheils sollst erblasen!
Licht meiner Hoffnung, leuchtet neu!
Ihr Engel, die mich einst verlassen,
stärkt jetzt dies Herz in seiner Treu'!

SENTA

Von mächt'gem Zauber überwunden,
reisst mich zu seiner Rettung fort.
Hier habe Heimat er gefunden!
Hier ruh' sein Schiff in sich' rem Port!
Was ist's, das mächtig in mir lebet,
Was schliesst berauscht mein Busen ein?
Allmächt'ger, was so hoch mich
erhebet,
lass es die Kraft der Treue sein!

DUTCHMAN

Ah, if you had any idea of the fate
that you would share with me,
you would be warned of the sacrifice
you make for me, if you swear to be
true.
Your youth would flee in horror
from the doom to which you consign it
if you do not have woman's most
beautiful virtue,
if you do not have eternal fidelity.

SENTA

I know well woman's sacred duty.
Take comfort, then, unhappy man.
Let destiny pass judgment on one
who can defy its decrees.
In the purest innocence of my heart
I know the highest demands of loyalty.
To whomever I give it, I give it
completely—
Faithfulness until death.

DUTCHMAN

A holy balm for my wounds
flows forth from your oath, from your
sacred words.
Hear this: my redemption I have found,
your powers that have struck me down.
You, star of my misfortune, will grow
pale.
Light of my hope, shine anew.
You angels, who once forsook me,
strengthen now this heart in its
faithfulness.

SENTA

By mighty magic overcome,
I feel compelled to rescue him.
Here may he find a home,
here may his ship rest safely in port.
What is this powerful feeling that lives in me?
What is it that fills my heart with ecstasy?
Almighty God, may that which raises me up
be the strength of my fidelity.

DALAND

Verzeiht! mein Volk hält draussen sich
nicht mehr.
Nach jeder Rückkunft, wisset, gibt's ein
Fest:
Verschönern möcht' ich's, komme
deshalb her,
Ob mit Verlobung sich's vereinen lässt?
Ich denk', Ihr habt nach Herzenswunsch
gefreit?
Senta, mein Kind! Sag', bist auch du
bereit?

SENTA

Hier meine Hand! und ohne Reu'
bis in den Tod gelob' ich Treu'!

HOLLÄNDER

Sie reicht die Hand!
Gesprochen sei Hohn, Hölle, dir, durch
ihre Treu'!

DALAND

Euch soll dies Bündnis nicht gereu'n!
Zum Fest!
Heut' soll sich alles freu'n!

DALAND

(Returning.)

Forgive me! My people will wait
outside no longer.
After each homecoming, you know, we
have a feast.
How proud I would be, if I could tell
them here
that you have agreed to a wedding.
I think your heart's wish has been
fulfilled?
Senta, my child, say if you are willing?

SENTA

Here is my hand. And without regret
I swear to be faithful until death.

DUTCHMAN

She gives her hand! May you be
scorned,
Hell, through her faithfulness.

DALAND

Neither of you will regret this union.
To the feast. Today, everyone will
rejoice!

AKT III

NORWEGISCHEN MATROSEN

Steuermann! Lass die Wacht!
Steuermann! Her zu uns!
Ho! He! Je! Ha!
Hisst die Segel auf! Anker fest!
Steuermann, her!
Fürchten weder Wind noch bösen
Strand,
Wollen heute 'mal recht lustig sein!
Jeder hat sein Mädel auf dem Land,
Herrlichen Tabak und guten
Branntwein!
Hussassahe! Klipp' und Sturm
drauss'—
Jollo ho he!—lachen wir aus!
Hussassahe! Segel ein! Anker fest!
Klipp'und Sturm lachen wir aus!
Steuermann, lass die Wacht!
Steuermann, her zu uns!
Ho! He! Je! Ha!
Steuermann, her! Trink mit uns!
Ho! He! Je! Ha!
Klipp und Sturm—he!—sind vorbei,
He! Hussahe! Hallohe! Hussahe!
Steuermann! He!
Her, komm' und trink' mit uns!

MÄDCHEN

Mein, seht doch an! Sie tanzen gar!
Der Mädchen bedarf's da nicht,
fürwahr!

MATROSEN

He! Mädel! Halt! Wo geht ihr hin?

MÄDCHEN

Steht euch nach frischem Wein der
Sinn?
Eu'r Nachbar dort soll auch 'was haben!
Ist Trank und Speis' für euch allein?

ACT III

(The harbour, at night. Daland's ship is lit up, and its crew are dancing and singing on board. Close to it is the Dutchman's ship, dark and silent.)

NORWEGIAN SAILORS

Helmsman, leave your watch!
Helmsman, come and join us.
Ho! He! Ye! Ha!
Furl the sail! Anchor fast!
Helmsman, here.
We fear neither wind nor treacherous
shore,
today we're going to be really merry.
Everyone has his girl here on land,
splendid tobacco and good brandy.
Hussassahe!
Reefs and storms outside—
Yollolohe!
we laugh at them!
Hussassahe!
Sail furled, anchor fast,
reef and storms we laugh away.

(The sailors dance on deck. The girls come to the quayside with food and wine.)

GIRLS

My, look at that! They're dancing
alone.
Girls are not needed here at all.

SAILORS

Hey, girls, stop! Where are you going
off to?

GIRLS

You're not the only ones with a taste
for cool wine.
Your neighbours there shall have some,
as well.
Do you think the food and drink is for
you alone?

STEUERMANN	HELMSMAN
Fürwahr! Tragt's hin den armen Knaben! Vor Durst sie scheinen matt zu sein.	Certainly! Take some to the poor fellows. They seem to be weak with thirst.
MATROSEN	SAILORS
Man hört sie nicht.	You can't hear them.
STEUERMANN	HELMSMAN
Ei seht doch nur! Kein Licht, von der Mannschaft keine Spur!	But, look, there's no light! Not a sign of the crew!
MÄDCHEN	GIRLS
	(Calling to the Dutch ship:)
He! Seeleut'! He! Wollt Fackeln ihr? Wo seid ihr doch? Man sieht nicht hier!	Hey, sailors! Do you want lights? Where are you, then? We can't see anything here.
MATROSEN	SAILORS
	(Laughing.)
Hahaha! Weckt sie nicht auf! Sie schlafen noch!	Don't wake them, they're still asleep.
MÄDCHEN	GIRLS
He! Seeleut'! He! Antwortet doch!	Hey, sailors! Answer us!
	(Silence.)
MATROSEN	SAILORS
Haha! Wahrhaftig, sie sind tot; Sie haben Speis' und Trank nicht not!	Haha! Truly, they are dead. They have no need of food and drink.
MÄDCHEN	GIRLS
Ei, Seeleute, liegt ihr so faul schon im Nest? Ist heute für euch denn nicht auch ein Fest?	Hey, sailors, why are you lying so lazily in your nest? Isn't today a feast for you, too?
MATROSEN	SAILORS
Sie liegen fest auf ihrem Platz, Wie Drachen hüten sie den Schatz.	They're staying right where they are, like dragons guarding treasure.

MÄDCHEN

He! Seeleute, wollt ihr nicht frischen
Wein?
Ihr müsset wahrlich doch durstig auch
sein!

MATROSEN

Sie trinken nicht, sie singen nicht!
In ihrem Schiffe brennt kein Licht.

MÄDCHEN

Sagt, habt ihr denn nicht auch ein
Schätzchen am Land?
Wollt ihr nicht mit tanzen auf
freundlichem Strand?

MATROSEN

Sie sind schon alt und bleich statt rot,
Und ihre Liebsten, die sind tot!

MÄDCHEN

He! Seeleut'! Seeleut', Wacht doch auf!
Wir bringen euch Speis' und Trank zu
Hauf!'

ALLER

He! Seeleut'! Seeleut'! Seeleut'!
Wacht doch auf! Wacht doch auf! *etc.*

MÄDCHEN

Wahrhaftig, ja! Sie scheinen tot!
Sie haben Speis' und Trank nicht not.

MATROSEN

Vom fliegenden Holländer wisst ihr ja!
Sein Schiff, wie es leibt, wie es lebt,
seht ihr da!

MÄDCHEN

So weckt die Mannschaft ja nicht auf!
Gespenster sind's, wir schwören drauf!

GIRLS

Hey, sailors, don't you want some cool
wine?
Surely you must be thirsty now?

SAILORS

They don't drink, they don't sing,
and there's no light burning in their
ship.

GIRLS

Tell us, haven't you got sweethearts
ashore?
Don't you want to dance with them on
the friendly shore?

SAILORS

They're old and pale, not ruddy,
and, as for their sweethearts, they're
dead.

GIRLS

Hey, sailors! Sailors! Wake up!
We've brought you lots of food and drink.

(*A long silence.*)

ALL

Hey, sailors, sailors! Wake up!

(*Silence still.*)

GIRLS

Truly, it seems they are dead.
They have no need of food and drink.

SAILORS

You've heard of the Flying Dutchman!
You see there the very image of his
ship!

GIRLS

That's why the crew do not wake up.
They're ghosts, we'd swear to it!

138

MATROSEN

Wieviel hundert Jahre schon seid ihr
zur See?
Euch tut ja der Sturm und die Klippe
nicht weh!

MÄDCHEN

Sie trinken nicht, sie singen nicht,
In ihrem Schiffe brennt kein Licht.

MATROSEN

Habt ihr keine Brief', keine Aufträg'
für's Land?
Unsern Urgrossvätern wir bringen's zur
Hand!

MÄDCHEN

Sie sind schon alt und bleich statt rot,
Und ihre Liebsten, ach! sind tot!

MATROSEN

Hei! Seeleute, spannt eure Segel doch
auf!
Und zeigt uns des fliegenden
Holländers Lauf!

MÄDCHEN

Sie hören nicht! Uns graust es hier!
Sie wollen nichts, was rufen wir?

MATROSEN

Ihr Mädel, lasst die Toten ruh'n!
Lasst's uns Lebend'gen gütlich tun!

MÄDCHEN

So nehmt! Der Nachbar hat's
verschmäht!

STEUERMANN UND MATROSEN

Wie? Kommt ihr denn nicht selbst an
Bord?

SAILORS

For how many centuries have you been
at sea?
Storms and reefs can do you no harm.

GIRLS

They don't drink, they don't sing,
and there's no light burning in their
ship.

SAILORS

Have you no letters, no messages for
people on shore?
We'll see they get to our great-
grandfathers!

GIRLS

They're already old and pale, not ruddy,
and their sweethearts, alas, are dead.

SAILORS

Hey, sailors, spread your sails,
and show us the Flying Dutchman's
speed.

GIRLS

They don't hear. It scares us here!
They don't want anything—why do we
call them?

SAILORS

Come on girls, leave the dead in peace.
Let us, the living, have some fun!

GIRLS

*(Giving their baskets of food and wine to the
sailors:)*

Take it! Your neighbour has scorned it!

HELMSMAN AND SAILORS

What? Aren't you coming on board
yourselves?

MÄDCHEN

Ei, jetzt noch nicht! Es ist ja nicht spät.
Wir kommen bald. Jetzt trinkt nur fort!
Und, wenn ihr wollt, so tanzt dazu.
Nur gönnt dem müden Nachbar Ruh'.

MATROSEN

Juchhe! Da gibt's die Fülle!
Lieb' Nachbar, habe Dank!

STEUERMANN

Zum Rand sein Glas ein jeder fülle!
Lieb' Nachbar liefert uns den Trank!

MATROSEN

Hallohohoho!
Lieb' Nachbarn, habt ihr Stimm' und
Sprach',
So wachet auf, und macht's uns nach!
Wachet auf! Wachet auf!
Auf! Macht's uns nach!
Hussa!
Steuermann! Lass die Wacht!
Steuermann! Her zu uns!
Ho, he, je, ha!
Hisst die Segel auf! Anker fest!
Steuermann, her!
Wachten manche Nacht bei Sturm und
Graus,
Tranken oft des Meer's gesalzenes Nass;
Heute wachen wir bei Saus und
Schmaus,
Besseres Getränk gibt Mädel uns vom
Fass!
Hussassahe! Klipp' und Sturm
draus'—
Jollolohe! Lachen wir aus!
Hussassahe! Segel ein! Anker fest!
Klipp' und Sturm lachen wir aus!

GIRLS

Oh, not yet. It's still quite early.
We'll come back soon. Drink up now
and dance too, if you want to.
Only let your weary neighbours rest!
Let them rest!

(They leave.)

SAILORS

Hurray! There's lots here!
Dear neighbours, thank you!

HELMSMAN

Everyone fill his glass to the brim!
Our dear neighbours have given us this
wine.

SAILORS

Halloho!
Dear neighbours, if you have voices and
speech,
wake up and do as we do.
Hussa!
Helmsman, leave your watch!
Helmsman, come and join us.
Ho! Ye! He! Yo!

Furl the sail! Anchor fast!
Helmsman, here.
We've watched many a night in fearful
storms,
we've often drunk the salty brine of the
sea;
today we watch with feasting and
revelling,
and the girls give us a better drink from
the cask.
Hussasahe!
Reefs and storms have gone.
Yollohohe!
We laugh them away.
Hussasahe!
Sails furled, anchor fast,
Reefs and storms we laugh away.

(The sea, otherwise calm, begins to heave around the Dutchman's ship, and a violent wind whistles through the rigging. A faint, blue flame illuminates the hitherto invisible crew.)

MANNSCHAFT DES HOLLÄNDERS

Jo ho hoe! Jo ho hoe! Hojo ho hoe!
Hoe! Hoe! Hoe! Hoe! Hoe!
Hoe! Hoe! Huissa!
Nach dem Land treibt der Sturm,
Huissa! Segel ein! Anker los!
Huissa! In die Bucht laufet ein!
Schwarzer Hauptmann, geh' and Land!
Sieben Jahre sind vorbei!
Frei' um blonden Mädchens Hand!
Blondes Mädchen, sie ihm treu'!
Lustig heut, hui!
Bräutigam! Hui!
Sturmwind heult Brautmusik,
Ozean tanzt dazu!
Hui! Horch, er pfeift! Kapitän!
Bist wieder da? Hui! Segel auf!
Deine Braut—sag, wo sie blieb?
Hui! Auf, in See!
Kapitän! Kapitän! Hast kein Glück in der Lieb'!
Hahaha! Sause, Sturmwind, heule zu!
Unsern Segeln lässt du Ruh'!
Satan hat sie uns gefeit,
Reissen nicht in Ewigkeit!

DUTCHMAN'S CREW

Yohohe! Yohohe! Hoe! Hoe! Hoe!
Huissa!
Towards land drives the storm—
Huissa!
In with the sail, anchor away!
Huissa!
Put into the bay!
Dark captain, go ashore,
seven years have passed.
Seek a blonde maiden's hand.
Blonde maiden, be true to him.
Be merry today,
bridegroom!
The stormy wind howls the wedding march—
The ocean dances to it.
Hui! Listen, he whistles!
Captain, you're back again?
Hui! Hoist the sail!
Your bride, tell us where she is.
Hui! Away, to sea!
Captain, Captain, you have no luck in love.
Hahaha!
Rage and roar, stormy wind!
You cannot disturb our sails.
Satan has bewitched them,
and they will not tear, for all eternity.

(During their song, a violent storm has raged around the Dutchman's ship, but everywhere else it is calm.)

NORWEGISCHEN MATROSEN

Welcher Sang! Ist es Spuk? Wie mich's graut!
Stimmet an! Unser Lied! Singet laut!
Steuermann, lass die Wacht!

NORWEGIAN SAILORS

What singing! Are they spooks?
How I tremble. Let's sing—
our song! Sing loud!
Helmsman, leave your watch! (etc.)

MANNSCHAFT DES HOLLÄNDERS

Sause, Sturmwind, heule zu, . . .

ERIK

Was musst' ich hören! Gott, was musst'
ich seh'n!
Ist's Täuschung? Wahrheit? Ist es Tat?

SENTA

O, frage nicht! Antwort darf ich nicht
geben!

ERIK

Gerechter Gott! Kein Zweifel, es ist
wahr!
Welch' unheilvolle Macht riss dich
dahin?
Welche Gewalt
verführte dich so schnell,
Grausam zu brechen dieses treu'ste
Herz!
Dein Vater, ha! den Bräut'gam bracht' er
mit,
Wohl kenn' ich ihn, mir ahnte, was
geschieht!
Doch du—ist's möglich!—
Reichest deine Hand dem Mann,
Der deine Schwelle kaum betrat!

SENTA

Nicht weiter! Schweig'!
Ich muss! Ich muss!

ERIK

O des Gehorsams, blind wie deine Tat!
Den Wink des Vaters nanntest du
willkommen,
Mit einem Stoss vernichtest du mein
Herz!

142

DUTCHMAN'S CREW

Rage and roar, stormy wind! (etc.)

(The song of the Dutchman's crew
overwhelms that of the Norwegian sailors,
who flee from the quay in terror, at which the
Dutchman's crew burst into scornful laughter.
Suddenly, their ship becomes deathly still
again, and the sea and sky become completely
calm.)

(Senta enters, followed by Erik.)

ERIK

What have I heard? What have I seen?
Is it illusion? Truth? Is it a fact?

SENTA

Oh, do not ask. I must not answer you.

ERIK

Almighty God! There's no doubt, it is
true!
What evil power has torn you away?
What power seduced you so quickly,
to make you cruelly break my trusting
heart?
Your father—he brought the
bridegroom with him—
I know him well, I guessed what would
happen.
But you—is it possible—you give your
hand
To a man who has hardly crossed your
threshold.

SENTA

No more! Be silent! I must, I must!

ERIK

Oh, such obedience—blind, just like
your deed!
You gladly obey a nod of your father's
head,
and with one blow you crushed my heart.

SENTA

Nicht mehr! Nicht mehr!
Ich darf dich nicht mehr seh'n,
Nicht an dich denken:
Hohe Pflicht gebeut's!

ERIK

Welch' hohe Pflicht? Ist's höh're nicht,
Zu halten, was du mir einst gelobst,
Ewige Treue?

SENTA

Wie? Ew'ge Treue hätt' ich dir gelobt?

ERIK

Senta! O, Senta! Leugnest du?
Willst jenes Tags du nicht dich mehr
entsinnen,
Als du zu dir mich riefest in das Tal?
Als, dir des Hochlands Blume zu
gewinnen,
Mutvoll ich trug Beschwerden ohne
Zahl?
Gedenkst du, wie auf steilem Felsenriffe
Vom Ufer wir den Vater scheiden
sah'n?
Er zog dahin auf weissbeschwingtem
Schiffe,
Und meinem Schutz vertraute er dich
an,
Als sich dein Arm um meinem Nacken
schlang,
Gestandest du mir Liebe nicht auf's
neu'?
Was bei der Hände Druck mich hehr
durchdrang,
Sag', war's nicht die Versich'rung
deiner Treu'?

HOLLÄNDER

Verloren! Ach! Verloren!
Ewig verlor'nes Heil!

SENTA

No more! No more! I must not see you
any more,
must not think of you. A higher duty
calls me.

ERIK

What higher duty? Is it not a higher
duty
to keep the promise you made me, to be
always true?

SENTA

What? Did I promise to be always true
to you?

ERIK

Senta, oh Senta, do you deny it?
Do you no longer remember the day
when you called me to you in the
valley?
when, to gather highland flowers for
you,
I took such risks without caring?
Do you remember how, from a steep
cliff,
we watched your father sail from the
harbour?
His ship sailed on, its white wake
spread behind,
and to my protection he entrusted you.
Then, as you put your arm around my
neck,
did you not pledge love to me anew?
The thrill that went through me at the
touch of your hand,
say, was it not the assurance of your
fidelity?

*(The Dutchman has entered, unobserved. Now
he comes forward, greatly agitated.)*

DUTCHMAN

Lost, ah, lost!
Salvation forever lost!

143

ERIK

Was seh' ich! Gott!

DUTCHMAN

Senta! leb' wohl!

SENTA

Halt' ein! Unsel'ger!

ERIK

Was beginnst du?

HOLLÄNDER

In See! In See!
In See für ew'ge Zeiten!
Um deine Treue ist's getan,
Um deine Treue, um mein Heil!
Leb'wohl! Ich will dich nicht verderben!

ERIK

Entsetzlich! Dieser Blick!

SENTA

Halt ein! Von dannen sollst du nimmer
flieh'n!

HOLLÄNDER

Segel auf! Anker los!
Sagt Lebewohl auf Ewigkeit dem Lande!

SENTA

Ha, zweifelst du an meiner Treue?
Unsel'ger, was verblendet dich?
Halt' ein! Das Bündnis nicht bereue!
Was ich gelobte, halte ich.

ERIK

Was hör' ich? Gott! Was muss ich sehen!
Muss ich dem Ohr, muss ich dem Auge
trau'n!
Senta! Willst du zu Grunde gehen?
Zu mir! zu mir! Du bist in Satans Klau'n!

ERIK

What do I see? Oh God!

DUTCHMAN

Senta, farewell!

SENTA

Wait, unhappy man!

ERIK

(To Senta:)

What are you doing?

DUTCHMAN

To sea! To sea—for all eternity!
It is the end of your fidelity—
of your fidelity—of my salvation!
Farewell, I will not destroy you!

ERIK

Oh, horror! That look of his!

SENTA

Stop! You shall never flee from here!

DUTCHMAN

Hoist the sails! Weigh anchor!
Say farewell for ever to land.

SENTA

Ha! Do you doubt my faithfulness?
Unhappy man, what has blinded you?
Stay! Do not regret our union!
The promise I made I will keep!

ERIK

What do I hear? God, what am I forced
to see?
Can I trust my ears, my eyes?
Senta, do you want to destroy yourself?
Come to me! You are in Satan's clutches!

144

HOLLÄNDER

Fort auf das Meer treibt's mich auf's
neue!
Ich zweifl' an dir! Ich zweifl' an Gott!
Dahin, dahin ist alle Treue!
Was du gelobtest, war dir Spott!
Erfahre das Geschick, vor dem ich dich
bewahr'!
Verdammt bin ich zum grässlichsten der
Lose,
Zehnfacher Tod wär' mir erwünschte
Lust!
Vom Fluch ein Weib allein kann mich
erlösen,
Ein Weib, das Treu' bis in den Tod mir
hält.
Wohl hast du Treue mir gelobt,
Doch vor dem Ewigen nicht: dies rettet
dich!
Denn wiss', Unsel'ge, welches das
Geschick
Das jene trifft, die mir die Treue
brechen:
Ew'ge Verdammnis ist ihr Los!
Zahllose Opfer fielen diesem Spruch
durch mich:
Du aber sollst gerettet sein! Leb' wohl!
Fahr' hin, mein Heil, in Ewigkeit!

ERIK

Zu Hilfe! Rettet, rettet sie!

SENTA

Wohl kenn' ich dich!
Wohl kenn' ich dein Geschick!
Ich kannte dich, als ich zuerst dich sah!
Das Ende deiner Qual ist da:
Ich bin's, durch deren Treu'
Dein Heil du finden sollst!

DUTCHMAN

Away to sea I am driven once more!
I no longer trust you, I no longer trust
God!
Gone, gone is all faithfulness!
What you promised was a joke to you!

Now learn the fate from which I shield
you!
I am condemned to the most dreadful
fate,
compared to which a ten-fold death
would be a great joy.
Only a woman can deliver me from this
curse,
a woman who would be true to me until
death.
You have indeed promised to be
faithful, but not
before God—that saves you!
For learn, unhappy girl, the fate of
those
who break their faith with me—
Eternal damnation is their lot!
Countless victims have suffered this fate
through me. But you shall be saved!
Farewell! And salvation, farewell for
eternity!

ERIK

*(Terrified, calls for help from Daland's house
and his ship.)*

Help! Save her, save her!

SENTA

(Trying to stop the Dutchman.)

I know you well! I know your fate
well!
I knew you when I first saw you!
The end of your suffering is near. I am
she
through whose faithfulness you shall
find salvation!

ERIK

Helft ihr! Sie ist verloren!

DALAND, MARY, GIRLS, SAILORS

Was erblick' ich! Gott!

HOLLÄNDER

Du kennst mich nicht, du ahnst nicht,
wer ich bin!
Befrag' die Meere aller Zonen,
Befrag' den Seemann, der den Ozean
durchstrich:
Er kennt dies Schiff, das Schrecken aller
Frommen:
Den fliegenden Holländer nennt man
mich.

MARY, ERIK, DALAND, MÄDCHEN,
MATROSEN

Senta! Senta! Was willst du tun?

MANNSCHAFT DES HOLLÄNDERS

Hoe! Hoe! Hoe! Huissa!

SENTA

Preis' deinen Engel und sein Gebot!
Hier steh' ich, treu dir bis zum Tod!

ERIK

Help her! She is lost!

MARY, DALAND, GIRLS AND
SAILORS

What do I see!

DUTCHMAN

(To Senta:)

You know me not, you've no idea who
I am!
Ask the sea of all the world, ask
the seaman who has roamed the oceans.
He knows this ship, the terror of all
pious men:
I am known as the Flying Dutchman!

*(Swiftly, the Dutchman boards his ship,
which immediately puts out to sea. Senta
rushes towards the ship, but is restrained by
Daland, Erik and Mary.)*

MARY, DALAND, ERIK, GIRLS AND
SAILORS

Senta, Senta! What are you doing?

*(Senta manages to break free, and rushes to
the top of a cliff overhanging the sea. She calls
after the Dutchman:)*

DUTCH CREW
Hoe! Hoe! Hoe! Huissa!

SENTA

Praise your angel and his decree!
Here I stand, true to you till death!

*(She throws herself into the sea. Immediately,
the Dutchman's ship sinks beneath the waves.
In the glow of the rising sun, the transfigured
forms of the Dutchman and Senta are seen in
close embrace, rising from the wreck of the
ship and soaring upwards.)*

CURTAIN

Chronology
Major Compositions
Further Reading

Chronology

1813   (Wilhelm) Richard Wagner born on May 22, in Leipzig, son of Karl Friedrich Wilhelm Wagner, clerk to the city police, and his wife Johanna, though his paternity is not absolutely certain. Karl dies from typhus, November 22, and Johanna is befriended by the actor Ludwig Geyer, Richard's possible father.

1814   Wagner's mother marries Geyer, and the family moves to Dresden.

1821   Geyer dies and his younger brother takes Wagner's education in hand in Eisleben.

1822   Wagner returns to Dresden to study at the Kreuzschule, where he shows precocious interest in Greek tragedy.

1824   Develops enthusiasm for the music of Weber and learns to play the piano, preferring to strum melodies from operas instead of practising.

1825   Writes a poem commemorating the death of a schoolfellow which is published.

1826   Neglects studies to write a Shakespearean tragedy, *Leubald und Adelaide*.

1827   Moves to Leipzig.

1828   Inspired to teach himself composition by hearing Beethoven symphonies at the Gewandhaus.

1829   Sees Wilhelmine Schröder-Devrient in *Fidelio* and determines on an artistic career. He composes a piano sonata and a concert overture.

1830   Takes part in the Leipzig Revolution in September. His Overture in B flat is performed at the Leipzig theatre on Christmas Day, conducted by Heinrich Dorn, and received with derision.

1831   Enters Leipzig University, where he studies music formally for a year. He composes further concert overtures and works for solo piano.

1832   Composes a Symphony in C during the spring, visits Vienna in the summer, followed by Prague, where the Symphony is performed by students.

1833   The Symphony performed at the Gewandhaus on January 10, and favourably received. He abandons work on an opera, *Die Hochzeit*, to sketch out *Die Feen*. He is appointed chorus master at Würzburg.

1834   Completes *Die Feen*, but the projected Leipzig production falls through. (The opera eventually has its première in Munich, 1888.) The performance of Schröder-Devrient in *I Capuleti e i Montecchi* persuades him to follow the Italian rather than the German operatic style. He publishes his first prose works, the articles 'The German Opera' and 'Pasticcio'. His appointment as conductor at Magdeburg brings him into contact with the actress Minna Planer. He writes the text of *Das Liebesverbot* and begins composing the music, abandoning work on a second symphony.

1835   His *Columbus* Overture performed at the Magdeburg theatre and at the Leipzig Gewandhaus. Minna Planer leaves for Berlin, but he sends her a formal proposal of marriage and she returns to Magdeburg.

1836   Completes the music of *Das Liebesverbot*, which is produced at Magdeburg for only two performances. Moves to Königsberg, where he marries Minna on November 24. He composes the *Rule, Britannia* Overture.

1837   Appointed conductor of the Königsberg theatre, which goes into liquidation after a few months. Meanwhile Minna leaves him to live with her parents in Dresden, and he petitions for divorce. He goes to Riga to take up a new conducting position, where he is shortly joined by Minna, with whom he has become reconciled.

1838   Busily engaged conducting a variety of operas, he nevertheless finds time to write the text of *Rienzi* and begin composing the music. He also conceives the first idea of *The Flying Dutchman*.

1839   Completes the first two acts of *Rienzi*. He is notified of his dismissal from the theatre in Riga, but leaves secretly before the appointed date to avoid creditors. After an illicit crossing of the Russo-Prussian border, he suffers a stormy sea voyage to London on his way to Paris. He meets Meyerbeer in Boulogne to seek his patronage, then reaches Paris on September 16.

1840   Endures great poverty in Paris, eking out a living by various forms of musical hack work. He also produces some of his most engaging prose works, including 'A Pilgrimage to Beethoven' for a Paris music journal, and completes the score of *Rienzi*.

1841   Sells the first libretto of *The Flying Dutchman* to the Paris Opéra, then writes a fuller 'poem' for his own use, completing the music by the end of the year.

1842   Leaves Paris on April 7 for Dresden, where he has been promised a production of *Rienzi* at the Court Theatre. *The Flying Dutchman* is provisionally accepted for production in Berlin. He makes a draft of the *Tannhäuser* libretto and sketches for some of the music. *Rienzi* produced in Dresden on October 20, with great success. He is appointed a conductor at the Court Theatre.

1843   *The Flying Dutchman* produced in Dresden on January 2, but is badly received and withdrawn after four performances. He completes the *Tannhäuser* poem and begins the music. *The Love Feast of the Apostles*, for male chorus and orchestra, is composed and performed.

1844   Completes the music of *Tannhäuser* except for the scoring. He delivers a notable oration at the Dresden burial of Weber's remains, which have been brought with great ceremony from London, and composes a funeral piece for eighty wind instruments and twenty muffled drums. He conducts *Rienzi* in Hamburg.

1845   Completes the scoring of *Tannhäuser*, conducting its performance at Dresden on October 19. During summer holiday at Marienbad he sketches a poem for *Die Meistersinger von Nürnberg* but lays it aside in favour of one for *Lohengrin*, which he completes before the end of the year.

1846   Conducts Beethoven's Ninth Symphony, which had been a great influence on him. He embarks on the music for *Lohengrin*, starting with Act III, during a holiday at Gross-Graupe, where he also meets Hans von Bülow, then aged 16.

1847   Composes the first two acts of *Lohengrin*. He arranges, conducts and produces Gluck's *Iphigénie en Aulide* at the Dresden Opera, where his dedication to the works of past masters wins him approval.

1848   Completes the scoring of *Lohengrin* in March, two months after the death of his mother. He writes the poem of *Siegfrieds Tod*. The political uprisings in Paris and Vienna early in the year prompt him to deliver an inflammatory speech at a political meeting, giving his local enemies the chance to brand him as a dangerous revolutionary. He becomes friendly with Liszt, whom he had previously disliked.

1849   Flees Dresden in May after the unsuccessful revolution there, going first to Weimar, where Liszt had presented *Tannhäuser* three months earlier. Hearing from Minna that a warrant for his arrest has been issued in Dresden, he seeks political asylum in Switzerland, settling in Zürich at the end of June. He writes 'The Art-Work of the Future'.

1850   Makes another unsuccessful attempt to establish himself in Paris, then in Bordeaux plans to leave Minna for ever. He arranges to elope with an Englishwoman, Jessie Laussot, but she decides at the last moment to remain with her husband. He settles down again in Zürich with the forgiving Minna. Liszt conducts the première of *Lohengrin* at Weimar on August 28, which Wagner cannot attend.

1851   Writes 'Opera and Drama' and 'A Communication to My Friends' as well as the poem for *Der junge Siegfried*. He next decides to expand his two *Siegfried* poems into a cycle of music dramas based on the Nibelungen Saga.

1852   Makes friends in Zürich with Otto Wesendonck, a wealthy patron of the arts, and his wife Mathilde. Writes the poems of *Das Rheingold* and *Die Walküre* and recasts the two other poems into *Siegfried* and *Götterdämmerung*.

1853   Works on the music of *Das Rheingold* and also composes an Album Sonata (for piano) dedicated to Mathilde Wesendonck. He visits Paris with Liszt, whose daughter Cosima he meets for the first time, and writes 'Remarks on Performing *The Flying Dutchman*'.

1854   Completes the full score of *Das Rheingold*, and composes the music for *Die Walküre* except for the scoring. While Minna is visiting Germany he begins a love affair with Mathilde which inspires him to thoughts of *Tristan und Isolde*. He reads Schopenhauer, whose philosophical ideas influence him considerably.

1855   Conducts a series of eight concerts in London to an enthusiastic public but a hostile press. He returns to Zürich to continue work on *Die Walküre*.

1856   Completes the scoring of *Die Walküre* and begins the music of *Siegfried*. He also writes a sketch for a Buddhist music drama.

1857   Finishes Act I and part of Act II of *Siegfried*, but lays it aside to write the poem of *Tristan und Isolde*. He moves to the Asyl in the grounds of the Wesendoncks' home and composes songs to words by Mathilde. He completes the music for Act I of *Tristan und Isolde* and begins thinking seriously of *Parsifal*.

1858 Scores Act I of *Tristan und Isolde* and composes the music for Act II. Minna, jealous of Mathilde, returns to Germany. He renounces Mathilde and goes to Venice, where he resumes composition.

1859 Completes *Tristan und Isolde* at Lucerne, then goes to Paris to negotiate the production of *Tannhäuser*. Minna returns to him, having tried to secure him an amnesty in Dresden.

1860 Prepares the Paris version of *Tannhäuser*. He is given permission to enter all the German states except the kingdom of Saxony, and visits Baden-Baden.

1861 *Tannhäuser* given in Paris, the first performance without incident but the second and third with such displays of hooliganism by the Jockey Club that he withdraws the work in disgust. He goes to Vienna to hear *Lohengrin* for the first time. Minna breaks with him finally. He visits the Wesendoncks in Venice, and is so stirred by Mathilde's enthusiasm for his idea of *Die Meistersinger von Nürnberg* that he writes the poem at great speed.

1862 Begins work on the music of *Die Meistersinger von Nürnberg*. He has a love affair with Friederike Meyer. An amnesty gives him freedom to go to Saxony again. Concerts of extracts from his works are given in Leipzig and Vienna.

1863 Gives concerts in Prague, St. Petersburg and Moscow in order to raise money for his ever-mounting debts. Returns to Vienna.

1864 Leaves Vienna to escape imprisonment for debt. He is invited to Munich by the 19-year-old Ludwig II of Bavaria, who offers him friendship and ideal conditions for producing his works. Wagner has Hans von Bülow appointed conductor at Munich and falls in love with his wife Cosima, the daughter of Liszt.

1865 Isolde, the daughter of Wagner and Cosima, is born in Munich on April 10. *Tristan und Isolde* receives its première in Munich on June 10, conducted by Bülow. Wagner's enemies persuade Ludwig to send him away from Munich. He goes again to Switzerland.

1866 Acts I and II of *Die Meistersinger von Nürnberg* finished. Cosima comes to Switzerland to join him, and they set up house at Triebschen on Lake Lucerne. Bülow visits them to silence the general gossip and agrees to a separation from Cosima. Wagner begins to dictate his autobiography, *Mein Leben*, to Cosima, but it is not published until 1911. Minna Wagner dies.

1867   Finishes composition of *Die Meistersinger von Nürnberg*, but not the orchestration. Another daughter, Eva, is born at Triebschen. They go to Munich for *Lohengrin* conducted by Bülow, whom Cosima joins for the sake of appearances.

1868   *Die Meistersinger von Nürnberg* premièred at Munich, with Bülow conducting, on June 21. Wagner and Cosima return to Triebschen, where he resumes composition on Act III of *Siegfried*. He meets Nietzshe on a visit to Leipzig.

1869   Completes *Siegfried* and begins to compose *Götterdämmerung*. *Das Rheingold* receives its premiere at Munich on September 22. A son, Siegfried, is born to Wagner and Cosima on June 6. She begins a diary of their life together which remains unpublished until 1976 in Germany, then two years later in English.

1870   *Die Walküre* premièred at Munich on June 26. He completes Acts I and II of *Götterdämmerung*. Cosima is divorced by Bülow in July and marries Wagner in August. The *Siegfried Idyll* is composed to celebrate Cosima's birthday and performed on the staircase at Triebschen on December 25. The idea of a festival theatre at Bayreuth begins to form in his mind.

1871   *Siegfried* fully scored. He pays a visit to Bayreuth, and considers it the ideal place for the building of the Festspielhaus. The first Wagner Society is formed, at Mannheim. He writes 'The Destiny of Opera'.

1872   Settles in Bayreuth, where the foundation stone of the theatre is laid on May 22, his birthday. He and Cosima visit Liszt, who became estranged from them when Cosima deserted Bülow. *Götterdämmerung* is now complete except for the scoring.

1873   Gives concerts again to raise funds for the theatre, including one on his sixtieth birthday featuring the youthful Symphony. The same day sees the beginning of the building of the Villa Wahnfried. Act I of *Götterdämmerung* completely orchestrated by Christmas Eve.

1874   Ludwig II comes to the rescue of the Festspielhaus with a huge donation when the whole scheme seems about to fail. The Wagners move into the Villa Wahnfried. The remainder of *Götterdämmerung* is fully orchestrated by November.

1875   Gives concerts in Berlin, Vienna and Budapest. Composes the Albumblatt in E flat. Assembles artists for the performance of *Der Ring des Nibelungen* in July.

1876   Supervises the first performance of *Der Ring des Nibelungen*, conducted by Richter, August 13–17. Three cycles are given, with immense artistic success but at an enormous financial deficit.

1877   Elaborates earlier sketches for *Parsifal*, publishes the complete poem, and begins the music. He goes to London to conduct eight concerts at the Albert Hall in aid of Bayreuth.

1878   Completes Acts I and II of *Parsifal* and begins the scoring. The first performance of *Der Ring des Nibelungen* outside Bayreuth is given at Leipzig.

1879   Composes Act III of *Parsifal*. He continues to write the essays on aesthetics which have occupied much of his energy for several years.

1880   Spends most of the year in Italy, at Naples, Perugia, Siena and Venice, finding the climate there better for his failing health.

1881   Acts I and II of *Parsifal* fully scored.

1882   Orchestration of *Parsifal* completed in Palermo. Its first performance is given at Bayreuth for patrons only on July 26, the first public performance on July 30. He leaves for Venice in September, suffering from sporadic heart attacks.

1883   Dies in Venice on February 13, and is buried at Bayreuth on February 18.

Major Compositions

Operas and Music Dramas
(Dates in brackets are those of first performances)

Die Hochzeit (unfinished)
Die Feen (1888)
Das Liebesverbot (1836)
Rienzi (1842)
Der fliegende Holländer (1843)
Tannhäuser (1845)
Lohengrin (1850)
Der Ring des Nibelungen
 Das Rheingold (1869)
 Die Walküre (1870)
 Siegfried (1876)
 Götterdämmerung (1876)
Tristan und Isolde (1865)
Die Meistersinger von Nürnberg (1868)
Parsifal (1882)

Orchestral Works

Symphony in C major
Concert Overture in D minor
Concert Overture in C major
Overture of *König Enzio*
Christoph Columbus Overture
Rule Britannia Overture
Polonia Overture
Eine Faust Ouvertüre
Huldigungsmarsch
Kaisermarsch
American Centennial March
Siegfried Idyll

Choral Works

An Webers Grabe
Das Liebesmahl der Apostel
Neujarhs-Kantate
National Hymn

Vocal

Wesendonck Lieder
Miscellaneous songs and arias

Piano Music

Sonata in B flat
Polonaise in D major (four hands)
Fantasia in F sharp minor
Album Sonata in E flat

Arrangements

Iphigenie en Aulide, revisions and additions to Gluck's opera
Piano and other arrangements of operas by Donizetti and Halévy

Further Reading

Goldman, Albert, and Sprinchorn, Evert (ed), *Wagner on Music and Drama* (London, 1977)

Jacobs, Robert L., *Wagner* (London, 1935)

Jacobs, Robert, and Skelton, Geoffrey (ed), *Wagner writes from Paris* (London, 1973)

Newman, Ernest, *The Life of Richard Wagner*, 4 Vols (London and New York, 1933–47)

Newman, Ernest, *Wagner as Man and Artist* (Revised Second Edition, New York, 1923)

Newman, Ernest, *Wagner Nights* (London, 1949)

Osborne, Charles, *Wagner and His World* (London, 1977)

Stein, Jack, *Richard Wagner and the Synthesis of the Arts* (Detroit, 1960)

Wagner, Cosima, *Diary*, Vol. I (London, 1978)

Wagner, Richard, *My Life* (London, 1911)

Acknowledgments

The illustrations are reproduced by kind permission of the following: Archiv für Kunst und Geschichte: 11, 13, 22, 29, 35, 70, 72; BBC Broadcasting House: 62, 85, 86, 87; Bettmann Archive: 66; Bildarchiv Preussischer Kulturbesitz: 20, 40–41, 43, 45, 46; Dell Publishing Co. Inc: 37; E. Piccagliani: 79, 80; Edo König—Bavaria: 65; EMI Limited: 105; Festspielleitung Bayreuth: 88, 89, 90, 101; H. Roger Viollet: 25, 75; Harold Rosenthal: 92–3; Houston Rogers: 6, 61, 106; Internat Bilder Agentur: 17, 31, 32; Internationale Bilderagentur, 103; Louis Mélancon: 55, 56, 77; Mander & Mitcheson Theatre Collection: 26, 34, 38; The Mansell Collection: 49, 50, 51; Mary Evans Picture Library: 69; Nancy Sorensen, 78; Radio Times Hulton Picture Library: 59; Robin May Collection: 52; Sedge Leblang: 73, 74; Sepp Bär: 98; Siegfried Lauterwasser—Bavaria: 95